ALEXANDRA
MUCH LOVE

BLESSINGS

The Art of Eloquence

Jeff Zaddick; The Fearless Poet

Understanding the communication prose

of your interdimensional divinity

The Art of Eloquence

Understanding the communication prose of your interdimensional divinity

First edition

Book one of

The Series of Divine Alchemy

as written by, Jeff Fosdick; The Fearless Poet

All rights reserved

Published by;
Wise Owl Shadow Press
1828 Carlson Rd
Snohomish, WA 98290

Find out more at

www.myfearlesspoet.com

Publisher's Cataloging-in-Publication Data

Names: Fosdick, Jeff, author.

Title: The art of eloquence : understanding the communication prose of your interdimensional
divinity / Jeff Fosdick.

Description: Snohomish, WA : Wise Owl Shadow Press, [2024] | Series: The series of divine

alchemy ; book one.

Identifiers: ISBN: 979-8-9874066-0-1 (Hardback) | 979-8-9874066-1-8 (E-book) | 979-8-

9874066-2-5 (Audiobook) | LCCN: 2023915246

Subjects: LCSH: Awareness. | Spirituality. | Spiritual formation. | Guardian angels. | Guides
(Spiritualism) | Mindfulness (Psychology) | Communication--Psychological aspects. |
Eloquence. | Extrasensory perception. | Vital force. | Psychic energy (Psychoanalysis)

Classification: LCC: BF311 .F67 2024 | DDC: 153--dc23

10 9 8 7 6 5 4 3 2 1

The Art of Eloquence

Table of contents

FOREWORD

The Art of Eloquence is the first of five books in Jeff Fosdick's Series of Divine Alchemy, a five-stage process of transformation to awakening us to our true selves. As such, it is the leading edge of a new way to help us achieve peace from the inside out as we make our way back to our perfect oneness with God, or as Jeff puts it "pathways to personal enlightenment." In this book, he gives us a highly practical guide to developing communication with Source, All-That-Is, God — whatever term you prefer to call that energy.

Known as the "Fearless Poet," Jeff was blessed in his early years with the gift of expressing spiritual concepts and guidance in simple, direct, poetic stanzas that are as beautiful as they are profound, yet easy to understand and follow. These stanzas form the backbone of each chapter in this and subsequent books. Over the years, I have personally observed him working with clients from many different backgrounds. Spiritual transformation can be approached from many different perspectives, but I have seen how much he helps people to improve the quality of their lives through his poetic readings and writing. As evidence of my respect for him and his work, on more than one occasion I have remarked to Jeff, "That was masterful!" He is, indeed, a "Fearless Poet" and a remarkable one at that.

Jeff Fosdick speaks with a wise voice that helps and inspires us to see that we are all naturally endowed with the gift of personal communion with Source energy. It is our birthright, ours to claim if we but awaken to our true selves. He helps us to see that all of our problems can, and ultimately must, be addressed on a spiritual level, which is the only place where we will find a lasting, and eventually permanent, solution to the challenges of daily life.

Dennis L. Dossett, PhD
Spiritual teacher and author of the three-volume Dancing with the Energy series

Preface

So now to tell the story, of how it came to be.
These universal teachings, so deep inside of me.
Listen to the echoes, the wisdom of the wind.
Inside this truth and light, it's here we now begin.

When I was a young boy, I always felt different, connected, a part of something greater. I remember times of joy; Christmas at grandma's, childhood horseback rides with my sister, running around the pool at my aunt's house, times I've fallen and couldn't get up on my own. There was always family to help pick me up and carry me on.

Somewhere in my early youth, a great deal changed. You see, I was on a predestined course to understand transition trauma. My family was very loving, kind, and close in all respects, yet between the ages of 8 and 18, I went through many of these transitions. In those 10 years, there were 18 major deaths in my life, many of them traumatic in their predisposition. This completely altered the course of my boyish reality. I became the jester in a way. I was gifted a connection with angelic balance and was taught to use comedy and goofiness to lighten those heavy hearts which surrounded me. At the age of 9, shortly after my eldest brother passed, the angels came and spoke to me—at first in my dreams. They started taking me places to see their realities, not to escape but simply comprehend the pain and ameliorate the perceived injustice of this tragic world I was living in. I have come to understand this space as a dimensional reference. I was being led through their meditative mindset, their castle, their safe space. The place where these angelic beings called home.

You see, the angels are very different from you and I. Rather than reintroduce negativity when they feel deeper emotions of abandonment, pain, grief, anger, or loss, they have a spot, a center, a zone, a room inside divinity to call their own where they can process these emotions before acting on anything negative in the case of their teachings inside of our current human understanding. This is the warm, loving place that "The Series of Divine Alchemy" will not only be based upon but lead you to. A place of absolute divinity and grace, of love and hope, of cherished blessings, and the understanding tone of absolute connection to the universal energy source.

It took a great deal of time, trial, and experience to fully understand the dimensional teachings that I will relay in these books. There are so many stories of seeing, feeling, and believing. I have been blessed with not only a personal understanding of the angelic realms yet also a high-functioning reading level since my early youth. These works are then a conglomeration of channeled angelic wisdoms, life experience, and the ability to study various books of history, culture, science, and spirituality. It is truly an angelically channeled series of divine alchemy.

A few years ago, I was completing a life mission. I had moved back into the house I was raised in to allow my parents to transition at the home they loved their family in. Near the completion of this mission, I heard my guides say, "It is time to put it all together." I was not sure what "it" was, yet I was willing to follow directions. I had been channeling angelic or divine essence poetry since my early childhood, and now, I was being asked to build a place to practice these conscious connections, a room to put them all together and study ancient aspects of worldwide spirituality, metaphysics, and energy movement. Having this format gifted to me by divine wisdom and grace, I developed and built a place in my home similar to the rooms I had observed in the Castle of Creation. I have come to term this place as "The Study." It is a crystal-activated room that works within the very highest vibrations on all aspects of science and spirituality. A meditation, writing, and reading area meant for channeling messages from the great divine.

Building the Study, I was met by guidance in every aspect. There were times when power tools and electric lights would not work properly, so the use of candles, oil lamps, and old hand tools was a necessity. Once the Study was in working order, the messages flowed like a river of conscious blessings. Angels and ancestors came to greet me, and I was reading, hearing, and interpreting many amazing things. I not only heard singing from my ancestors,

I experienced sights, visions, and comprehensions of divine intercession in both the words we were writing and the actions being taken. There are so many concepts and ideals that continue to flow each and every time I sit down for ceremony within this sacred space. On a late autumn evening, I was literally burning the midnight oil in the Study when something absolutely amazing happened. I got slapped in the back of the head. I was completely awestruck by this action as no human was around. I turned to see where this slap had come from, and for the first time, one of my oldest and dearest angel friends was physically standing in the Study.

He pointed a finger at me and stated. "Listen, this is what we are going to do!" He relayed messages that true artistry and elegance touch the realms of spirituality and dimension, that I had been given a gift to not only understand this but was also handed an activated sequence of teaching and relaying this information to others. He said that I was accessing psychic and spiritual guidance through the written word, and I was to start doing personal readings and activations wherever I could. He also said I was being handed an angelic pathway of understanding the individual essence of our innate human divinity, and I was supposed to write it all out in at least five books. This is the calling that continues to drive me forward at every moment.

I have been performing activated psychic guidance through channeled poetry for a few years now and have a growing list of classes, artwork, and guided meditations being introduced daily. There is also the knowledge of crystal energy vibrations, which I had originally started using intuitively as a healing tool for my mother in 1998. The stories continue to astound me. This connection to source, to spirit, to conscious activation of our divinely gifted reality—that is what I am here to speak about. This is the platform I get to teach and learn from inside our unified environment.

Throughout my life, I have met and learned from some very deeply rooted spiritual people, events, and interactions. There was the missionary family from my childhood church, some of which I am still in contact with today, and there are so many different indigenous peoples who I have had the honor of praying with and learning from. At one point, I was even afforded the opportunity to meet the Dalai Lama. The books I have read and the stories I could tell are so many and various that I could take up this whole book just writing the preface.

But we are here to talk about pathways to personal enlightenment. To achieve and understand what I have come to term as our greatest good. For that, we have to look further, deeper, more involved than any human psychological understandings we may have learned. We allow ourselves to look at our aspects of interpretation and communication within our universal blessings. Alluding to our psychology, we get to look at the powers of our nature and our nurture.

The one story that I would love to relay in this preface is a personal understanding of compassion, hope, joy, love, and grace. This was not only handed to me by the angels who guide and guard our existence but came as a physical representation through a starving animal.

A few years ago, I was in another space and time frame of this wonderful and beautiful existence. I was residing in a single-wide trailer in northern California, and next to the trailer was an abandoned house. The family who had abandoned the house had been raising dogs for fighting. When they left the domicile, they also abandoned their oldest breeding brindle female.

By the time I had moved into the trailer, she had not only birthed a litter of pups, but had run out of resources to feed or raise them. She would go out hunting every day in the fields of northern California, never trusting humans, as her life with them was one of pain, torture and continued agony. She was starving, and in turn, so were her babies. It was around the holidays, and I also was far from my family. There were a few people around who were treating me kindly and dropped off a great deal of holiday leftovers for me, much more than I would be able to eat before they turned bad so I decided the best course of action was to feed the starving dogs. I put together a huge platter and stacked it to the brim with turkey, gravy, mashed potatoes, and all the trimmings. I then took this platter and laid it in front of the hole where the mother had been going in and out from under the abandoned house. I walked about 15 feet away and made some whistles and kissing sounds saying here pup and the like.

About a minute passed, and the most curious thing happened. The mother appeared, still wary of me and my presence, she walked up to the huge plate of food, then she did the most amazing thing. This starving divine mother went back under the house without eating a bite. The waiting to see what would happen started, and it seemed to me like an eternity passed. There was more than enough for all of us to eat, enjoy, feel and be at once, happy and fulfilled.

Soon, the mother came back out of her hole, followed by the litter of seven pups. She led the pups to the platter, they surrounded it and went to town. Tails wagging with the joyful discovery of nourishment. Then the mother did the most inspiring and admirable thing. I have never seen this level of compassion, grace, of absolute understanding of life cycle, or true and unadulterated love. She walked away from the platter without eating a bite, she was letting her children have their fill. This was a starving animal. She was making sure her lineage would prevail above and beyond herself while knowing and understanding her imminent demise. I eventually grabbed a second plate from my kitchen and took a third of the leftovers which were piled well above the pups heads and their wagging little tails and set it out for this mother. She eventually came and ate. Yet here I was, left with this amazing understanding of hope, joy, love, and compassion for our fellows. They are so much more than I.

I would love to think that each person, on the face of our beautiful planet earth, innately has this level of compassion and awareness. I believe in the hope of our human and earthly divinity to reach out, to guide and guard every person, place, and thing we meet or come into contact with. To think, feel, and believe the very best in each and everything we see, touch, taste, feel, and interpret. It is with the understanding of these energies that this work was made possible. It is by being gifted many angelic understandings and scientific awareness of the quantum mind that this alchemization process of divine spirit could take place. I am truly a simple poet who has been gifted some education, experience, and a few bestowed blessings of interpretation and understanding. These gifts come from the Creator of our divinely gifted reality and it is within the here and now that I have been guided to share them with you.

Introduction to The Series of Divine Alchemy

To hear the ancient teachings, as a whisper on the air.
To balance out these echoes, and bring them all to bare.
Now introduce the system of what we see as life,
to find the fledgling feelings, which build our joy from strife.

The Series of Divine Alchemy. This was something I heard much later after having written the first draft of The Art of Eloquence. I was originally told to write at least five books on the adventures of balancing human spirit and engaging our divine potential. I was busy writing the first book, and it was challenging to finish the final editing process. I had the title nailed, but the subtitle just kept changing to reflect the direct intention of these works.

One day I was engaging in another creative endeavor and this conversation happened. I love how my guides and ancestors talk to me. When they are giving me direction and intuitive guidance, they treat me like I'm a kid. I am sure that is because I am to them. As I was editing the first book and looking to provide definition to the sequence and teachings, I heard, "How many books were you told to write?" I answered, "At least five," as that is what I had originally heard. Then they said, "You know it is a series, don't you?" I was dumbfounded.

Then I heard it was to be called "The Series of Divine Alchemy." The Series of Divine Alchemy is a living, five-stage process. This process brings us all to angelic understanding and guidance to be the very best of ourselves in each situation or endeavor which we encounter in our human existence. It leads us to and through the dimensions of divine grace, wisdom, and knowledge. This process is an opening of the light streams or living energy that create and define us all.

The initial understanding of communication with our divine energies and guidance is laid out in this first book. We get to learn divine communication as the fundamental guide point of where we are going and what we are here to accomplish in our three-dimensional existence. That is the activated reference of The Art of

Eloquence. How we, in our human understanding, can communicate with everything all at once. How to use our divine tools in every interaction as a guiding point for our universal or energetic beings and communicate these understandings with balance and grace. The aspect of personal omnipotence is a very tricky situation to describe. Still, we are as big as we are small. The first book will guide us in this caring and compassionate communication within the everything. In the first book, there is channeled poetry to define the teachings. In, The Art of Eloquence, I was asked to use the term "Bet" or "better." Bet, being the second letter of the Hebrew Aleph-Bet, it is termed as the number two, so every poem in this first book is the second or greater of the pieces written on any given day of a calendar year.

The second book is the daily activation process. The second book is titled The Book of Aleph, representing the number one or, in many definitions, termed as always silent. The second book is a course of daily meditations involving activated poetry to align ourselves within the divine essence of our beings. This allows us to bring true connection and understanding into our daily walks with care, compassion, and guidance. It brings us all to a point of communication or balance in a kind and gentle, nurturing way. This, after all, is how the divine energies communicate with us. In the second book, we get to engage the understanding of the without. What is out there besides the self? How do we interpret and understand the without and use it to the best of our abilities within?

The third book, Seasoned by the Trials, is the vision. It is a walk through the first nine dimensions and the sequence of that interpretation. This book is a Homeric-styled epic poem that describes and defines the beginning of our basic nine-dimensional structure. Picturesque in the essence of walking through our three-dimensional understandings into dimensions four, five, and six, where we engage our communication with our divine beings and various other energies and entities and where they reside as physical beings, much like you and I, in dimensions seven, eight, and nine. This is where my childhood visions started and angelic understandings were gifted to me. It is through their aspect of

Universal Love that I get to relay these messages to you. We are here as a direct channel or conduit of this divine energy. In the third book, we see what angelic or divine understanding desires us to interpret about our dimensional self. We become aware of the all, thus bridging us to the infinite loop of Within, Without, With All.

Book four is titled The Great Rewind, this theory originated before I received the title of the first book. When the greater aspects of our human consciousness arise to the point of angelic understanding and communication within our daily tasks, then social reconstruction will be paramount. We could not live in a fear-based society of judgment or condemnation surviving through personal guises of want or will. The aspect of social reconstruction will be freedom of expression, thought, and understanding. This book will speak to that reconstruction process. The Great Rewind gives every individual on our beautiful planet the understanding virtue of the freedom to be the very best of themselves.

The 5th book is the very first book which I was called to write. As a youth, I heard and channeled a poem named "A Call to Arts." This is an understanding of creation and how it continues to happen inside of our infinite loop. We are all artistic by nature. Our many gifts and ideals work together as one, to expand and enlighten our human horizons. Book five, or, A Call to Arts refers us to engage the greater aspects of our artistic understandings. There is artwork in every human endeavor—from the way we dress to the ways we design our architecture, the ways we move and flow within our elemental understandings. These are all a ray or hue of our personal artistic alignment. A Call to Arts engages this process of universal understanding that everything is creative. We all know, and it is by bringing our internal knowledge together for the greatest good that we arise together.

This is the foundation of guidance and blessing, the formative building blocks of understanding divine or angelic wisdom and grace. There are so many interpretations of spiritual energy and guidance. We could speak of Biblical, Tibetan, Egyptian, Sumerian, or even Essene understandings, amongst a great multitude of others. Cultures all over the world have their own individual versions of angelic or enlightened creators. The Series of Divine Alchemy will carry the prose that we are all enlightened creators. In any aspect of our human creation, we learn that we were created from two individual things. These things vary slightly from culture to culture, but to break them down to their essence, it has been stated that humans were created from the dust of the Earth and the breath of God.

We are all gifted children carrying the teachings of our Earthly Mother and our Heavenly father. It is by living in this wisdom and accountability we get to use our care, compassion and guidance for everything around us at all times. One of my favorite quotes comes from the Essene Gospel of Peace. It states that

"If anyone says, 'I love God,' yet hates [their] brother, [they are] a liar. For anyone who does not love [their] brother, whom [they have] seen, cannot love God, whom [they have] not seen."

It is with this love that I get to bring you the first book in The Series of Divine Alchemy. We will now begin learning the ways to communicate with

The Art of Eloquence

THE ART OF ELOQUENCE

To communicate with oneness, in everything and all.
To bring about the balance, of great and very small.
In the micro and the macro, hear the angels in the air.
As guide and guard and witness. To what we now will share.

Eloquence, let's take a look at that word. It has been defined as "a fluent, elegant, or persuasive style of communication, primarily the power of expressing strong emotions in striking and appropriate language." This is exactly how spirit speaks to and through us on a moment by moment basis. It is a respectful and balanced understanding not only of self-awareness, yet also how to communicate within the wondrous and beautiful powers of both nature and nurture.

The universe communicates this balance to us on a daily basis and we can see these aspects in our synchronicities and events. Not only are we determining our role or goal in life, there are guiding patterns of thought and analysis that shape our ideals and formulate options within our free will. Communication, then, is not only with our divine surroundings; it is deep within the oneness of self. We are our greatest teachers, biggest benefactors, and strongest adversaries. We—you and I—are not only the grounding force of divine energy and guidance; we are the balanced equation of infinite understanding. That is the relation of *The Art of Eloquence.*

So let's dive into this process. There are 14 elemental understandings taught in this book, each one building on the prior and used as a foundation for the next. The result is an activation or awakening as a spiritually balanced individual with the ability to not only understand our conscious downloads, yet still, to bring them into words or eloquate them. After this, we can interject thoughts and ideals into divine understanding with conscious intent.

The Art of Eloquence is a format or pathway to awareness of constant communication with the divine energies that surround us, encompass our existence, and move through us all in each and every moment. This 14-stage process starts at the formative building blocks of the self, as once we move through the aspect of understanding our dreams and visions, there are whole new realms of interpretation to be understood and developed. Then we can channel angelic understanding in a much clearer or broader perspective.The realization our divine beings are here to help and heal is paramount, that is why the chapters are structured in a specific order. We get to understand the spiritual self in humility or equanimity of where we are and what we are here to accomplish, then we meet our advisors on this path.

Once we start our conversations with these counselors, we begin to learn their interpretive languages. There are three separate aspects of universal communication and understanding laid out in this work. They each lay at separate and distinct intervals on the path of our spiritually balanced progression. Without the tools necessary for their incorporation with the self, these languages are hard to understand and nearly impossible to interpret. What we will be incorporating are the understandable aspects of empathic or telepathic light language. We are all built from the fabric of energy or light. Using that reference, we can begin to work inside of it to become the very best of ourselves and help and heal not only ourselves but everything that surrounds us.

The universe communicates with us through sound or as vibrations of emotions, and we can understand this through empathy. The ringing many get in their ears is usually a form of these sounds or vibrations as a chordal structure. Each note in the chord of creation builds on the next to produce a unified effect or action. It is by understanding the base, or fundamental being, we get to engage these aspects of emotional language and lead ourselves into the higher realms of divine creative thought.

Creation of anything is conceptual. The mind of any poet, actor, writer, or anyone with a sense of creativity works on another level of thought where passion lies in its purest form, where dimensions are separated only by the preconceived boundaries of one's ideology. There are currently many purveyors of knowledge and spirituality. Anyone can find any teaching they desire either in print, verbally, electronically, or in many instances, within states of prayer and meditation.There is a field, a creative source we should call it. It is a simple and pure energetic fluctuation. Inside of it are not only aspects of creation yet also echoes of guided, God-sent spiritual wisdoms, healing elements of both physical and emotional state, and vibrations which renew, invigorate, restore personal health and hold a vast array of wisdoms and laws.

I have heard many terms for this place. Some call it a field, a dimension, or even a Hall of Records. Many are guided in separate directions to their own pieces or parts of its beautiful wisdom. They then formulate individual theories and teach their intuitive knowledge of healing, creation, philosophy, spirituality, or whichever discipline they have been so called to interpret, discover, and translate. I am a simple poet who has touched all elements of this creative field. I have walked the hallways, shared, loved, cried, and felt both the exuberance and exhaustive index of this vibrational flow.

Years ago when I was first taken there by my guides, I called it a castle, as that is what I saw in my visions. I started writing divined spiritual poetry from this place at the age of 11. One of my earlier youthful pieces, or teenage trials as I like to call them, speaks of a castle on the hill where the angels come to cry. The creative flow from this dimensional space is available to anyone. Many see different and diverse aspects. They come with great explanations and wonderful teachings. This is all over books, print media, and the internet, in courses of meditation, compassion, honesty, and true spiritual natures.

I not only wish to hand you those beautiful building blocks of the humanitarian spirit but also assist everyone to unlock these doors for themselves. To see your own pathway, to follow your own guidance. It is in this way that we all evolve to live our own individuality while completing the oneness or infinite loop designed for us by the Creator. I am stating that no one is right, that everyone is right. That you are right, as you are right here and right now. That all things hold a delicate balance of everything, and it is with this understanding that we grow. We are all here with specific reason and purpose. The poetic formats I have been gifted fixates on many philosophies and wisdoms, too many to cover in a single manuscript, yet I have been given a course to follow by my angelic guides.

There are many avenues to teach people of personal

enlightenment: meditation, spirituality, the arts of inner energy flow, such as yoga or Tai Chi and all of these are wonderful and vital aspects of personal healing and overall vibrational enrichment. I, as a simple poet, am here to ask not only where does all this wisdom come from, yet how do I get there, and how can I show others to get there as well? How do I witness everything with both beauty and depravity, while knowing the pureness of balance from the natural standpoint, and most of all, how do I empower others to see and open these pathways for themselves? This is a book of poetry; this is a book of passion, of romance, of personal divinity and freedom from the constraints of self. Come along and talk to your angels, fly with your dragons, travel the universe to find and witness the goals we didn't know we had. Our possibilities are limitless. Let us open up perception and give it a taste!

There are a few theories I will cover from both a poetic or artistic standpoint, as well as an ideological or teaching platform. Let your mind wander, let your spirit soar, let your being open your individual pathway to enrichment of Universal wisdom and knowledge. That way when I am in need, you can teach me.

The touching of the fire,
the illuminating good.
As bright and bold desire,
lays burning in the wood.

The structure starts its shifting,
as the ground begins to sway.
The visions of our blessings,
now come to pass this way.

Upon a silent sunrise,
within a distant dream.
We strive to find a discourse,
with the world it would seem.

About the understanding,
which once could come to pass.
With hues of golden visions,
in greens of greenest grass.

Our heart is at a crossroads,
on a precipice of fate.
Let's strive to find the answers,
before it comes too late.

A hopefulness becomes me,
the language of my love.
It dances on the starlight,
it stems from God above.

That all may see the vision,
upon their passions hill,
And come to find the answers.
their Spirit if you will.

11/30/19
Gimel

This piece is truly an introduction to what I would like to accomplish with this book. It touches many aspects of the ideologies that are the spiritual essence on which we can all grow. It speaks well of passion from the elemental standpoint of fire. It talks of love and states all our blessings are everywhere around us, it is with this gratitude that we communicate with our Creator.

There is a point it makes over striving to find a discourse with everyone around us. Isn't that what each and everyone of us are doing? Tempting to find our own individual aspect of understanding and acknowledgment for our thoughts, impulses, and ideals. We are all spiritual beings leading a very human life. This is a wonderful and beautiful time to be alive.

We are at the precipice of the awakening of divine communication inside and throughout our infinite loop and time cycles. What a wonderful and blessed time it is to usher in this great awakening. Be this illumination of good. Touch your fire and let it be known to the world. Communicate your goodness in every aspect of your being. Treat each and every individual with the love and compassion that you so rightly deserve.

The philosophical aspect of watching the fire move and grow is how we as individuals change and learn over time. We see our blessings, yet do not completely understand what to do with them. Enjoy them, count them, much more, share them in your communications to the world around you. This is how we as a culture evolve to do our greatest good.

Welcome to this natural evolution of communication between our divine self and the creative consciousness. We will speak of how universal and dimensional thought theory and energy flow through each and everyone of us, how it prepares us for the work of harmonious transfer to reach the very best of ourselves on a moment-by-moment basis within all aspects of our humanity. Your visionary abilities, psychic awareness, and aptitude to communicate freely and be heard by the universe are in your hands right here and right now. As always, blessings and prayers. As the Essene mystics would say,

peace be with you!

Jeff
The Fearless Poet

The Art of Eloquence
14 stage sequence of personal activation

Chapter 1 Dreams
(The beginning of our personal awareness)

One of the reasons we get to look at dreams as a beginning of our base needs is because they are a foundation of our individual spiritual awareness. Think of it, were you not dreaming before you could read or write? A newborn child sleep roughly 14-17 hours a day on average. Their world is surrounded and built upon the foundation of dreams. As an infant, we understood or had lessons and communications from our dream state possibly before any parental teachings.

There have always been dreams involved in our spiritual makeup, even prior to our understanding of their worth or intent. The very first access we gain to our own unique individual spiritual guides are through dreams. It is up to us to assess that information, find its significance, and use it as a building block for our personal legacies and inner spiritual balance.

What are we trying to build or attain in our lives, and how can our dreams guide us that way? Many are looking to attain a certain point of enlightenment or just live a happy, productive, and fulfilling life. Our dreams are not only a solace or refuge of our everyday life, they are a fundamental building block of our individual healing and transformation. The dream state is a place where it is safe to eloquate our deepest desires and engage our greatest truths.

There is a great deal of emotional and psychological trauma that can be reviewed, edited, and counseled while in the dream state. There are dreams where we interact with spiritual or esoteric beings, as well as dreams of recent memories, coming events, or having supernatural abilities such as flight or fending off an overwhelming attacker to save our families. Many scientists and healers have studied dreams for years because of their fundamental importance in our lives. The understanding of them, the knowledge of how they work, and what process they serve are all paramount in identifying our own unique spirituality.

The spark we feel after waking up from a beautiful or poignant dream is a healing echo from our spiritual makeup. I remember shortly after my mom had passed. I had a dream where we actually had a quick conversation. We shared tears of joy with the understanding of being together again. We drew into a close proximity. The conversation led to the "I love you and miss you" phases. Then we embraced each other. As we did, I was shot awake, wishing I could go back to sleep to spend just another moment with my mother. Was this a lucid dream? Was it pent-up anxiety or agony? Or was it a message from the spiritual realm that my mother was okay, was still caring for me, and was watching over me, from another realm of existence?

There was also another very close representation in a dream my brother's wife had on the evening after my father had passed away in his sleep at their home. On the day his body was in bed awaiting transport, I was there to say my goodbyes. I asked my brother's wife if I could burn some things while making my final prayers over his physical body. Knowing me, she laughed and asked, "It's not like a Greek funeral effigy fire is it?" I replied, "No, I mean like some sage, incense, or even a candle."

She gave me that permission, and I got these objects with a large piece of rose quartz to signify the coming together of universal love. Then I cleaned and cleared the energy field around my father and prayed, with the candle and rose quartz, that he be unified with my mother. They had been married over 60 years at that point, and it was their desire to both be cremated and released together. I then took the extinguished candle and rose quartz tower and brought them to my mother's ashes, reignited the candle, and repeated the same unification prayer.

The next morning when I awoke, my brother informed me that his wife had the strangest dream where she went into my father's bedroom, after his body had been removed, to mourn and his body was returned under the covers. Excited and overjoyed, she exclaimed, "Pops, Pops, You came back to us," then yanked back the covers to see that his whole body was now made of pink quartz crystals. I laughed and told them both what I had done in my prayer ceremony over his body, letting them know with love that this was his way of telling us that he and mom were together again and that everything was going to be alright. So many tears, joys, and hugs were shared.

9

The healing natures of universal source is here an understanding and equate able format. I have many other personal stories about dream interpretation, how it affects us, and how we can learn from it in the multiple layers of our 3 dimensional realities.

Dreams are where we start on our pathway of understanding the divine and the great creative mysteries permeating our culture. Many mysticisms speak of the universal language and the unwritten law of God. The understanding of these pathways begins as a message in our dreams. Know your dreams. Learn to interpret their knowledge. In this way, we can balance the spiritual plane of existence with our individual human understanding in this physical realm.

There are a few pieces of poetry from the Study journals that define and give deeper activation into understanding the human dream state. We are all in this together. It is by sharing our diverse understanding with our faith in the divinity of human spirit that we can all grow and learn to communicate our truest selves to the divine world within and around us.

Dreams Artistic Impressions

1. 1/7/20 Dalet - A brief poetic passion

2. 2/27/20 Dalet - A simple draft of reason

3. Pre-Study - To dream about disturbance

4. 1/29/20 Hay - The beauty is becoming

5. 12/6/19 Hay - In sequences of vision

6. 12/7/19 Dalet - In vision and in sight

7. BC 1 - Don't quantify the echoes

8. 2/28/20 Bet - There's no such thing as sadness

9. 12/28/19 Chet - To facilitate the silence

10. 3/28/20 Dalet - Now shelter in the silence

A brief poetic passion,
a bright, entrancing joy.
A balance of a vision,
a man where once was boy.

Dreams draw drafts of discourse,
A thought to talk upon.
As we walk our pathway,
or sojourn fast along.

Our human rights and wishes,
may designate our power.
As time drops past our mindset,
yes quicker by the hour.

The clearness of the purity,
on the energy of light.
Now wells within our beings,
on each and every night.

1/7/20
Dalet

A simple draft of reason,
a ray of purest truth.
A wisdom for the ages,
sings through the hearts of youth.

With joy of just becoming,
and eagerness to learn.
We open up our mindset,
to see just what we yearn.

To chase it with a passion,
to live to love to dream.
To follow to fruition,
the romance of the scene.

When hearts beat one with likeness,
on any given day.
We see that our forever,
has brought us here to stay.

2/27/20
Dalet

To dream about disturbance,
of just the light of day.
To keep a solemn promise,
in each and every way.

When words are but a whisper,
on the moments of our fate.
We set the course for sunrise,
and try to contemplate.

With sight so out of sequence,
or is it just our dreams?
Are we drawn to distance,
to illustrate these scenes?

Aghast another heartbreak,
comes crashing to the ground.
To elevate this mindset,
to love what's all around.

Pre-Study Counter

The beauty is becoming,
what we were meant to be.
To truly find a fraction,
of our eternity.

In silence as in shadow,
within a distant light.
We ordain only empathy,
to perceive what is right.

A shelter of subsistence,
elapses over time.
A secret hidden treasure,
folds instantly in rhyme.

And so we're drawn to discourse,
with the depth upon the sky.
To emulate the energy,
of dreams in which we fly.

1/29/20
Hay

In sequences of vision,
or the series of a sight.
Now fall upon perception,
of what we know as right.

The task is now to equal,
the balance of our dreams.
To manifest their greatness,
in daily light routines.

So speak about your passion,
talk about what's real.
Fixate your foundation,
to find the love you feel.

With lights of purest intrigue,
so long about the day.
We burn with just compassion,
in all we do and say.

12/6/19
Hay

In vision and in sight.
now pouring out the soul.
We're vibrating on fields,
of a long-awaited goal.

To sit in certain concept,
of what has started here.
As abstract as this vision,
we've come to battle fear.

Each time we sit to conquer,
the demons of our dreams.
And bring to light the essence,
of what love surely means.

Now draft away on reason,
about a simple time,
Where everyone knows rhythm,
and every goal has rhyme.

12/7/19
Dalet

Don't quantify the echoes,
with the errors of your thought.
Don't give up on wisdom,
in the searches you have sought.

Keep watchful eye on daydreams,
within the constant storm.
As everywhere is beauty,
and nothing is the norm.

When words waft by the wayside,
in the ancient draft of Dreams.
And romance is a reason,
to find forevers means.

We see within the sequence,
that our passion has no end.
That even with no equal,
there is solace in the pen.

BL 1

There's no such thing as sadness,
there's no such thing as pain.
In clouds upon the sunrise,
there's no such thing as rain.

This eloquence eludes us,
evades our simple time.
To rant inside of rhythm,
or reason with a rhyme.

So sift away the shackles,
like the dust we tempt to sweep.
Clean those creature comforts,
in the sights within your sleep.

In longings of our luxury,
we stand for only greed.
With Creator as our council,
now gain the hope we need.

2/28/20
Bet

To facilitate the silence,
of a dawning century.
To remove the self from vision,
so we can finally see.

We sit upon a precipice,
of transparent human will.
To pray to the Creator,
that our thought may never still.

We dream of second chances,
they illuminate the sky.
And drive the cloud from vision,
on the secrecy of why.

So sensible is structure,
a warm protective glow.
Yet who will see forever,
and how are we to know?

12/28/19
Chet

Now shelter in the silence,
as there is no turning back.
The clock upon the wall,
or the tightness coming slack.

To sit upon a symptom,
of a mercy in our mind.
And silhouette the shadow,
with the sequence that we find.

We've promised you perfection,
As a feather touches air.
We've riddled it with impulse,
and tried so much to share.

So here we are just waiting,
on the dawning of your dream.
To find the brightened passage,
to the silence of our scream.

3/28/20
Dalet

The first step of communicating within inter dimensional divinity is to understand our dreams. To think about our dreams, we must ask ourselves where do these insights come from? Who brings them to our subconscious and delivers them to the conscious interaction of our thought? Are they gifts from the Dios of another level of existence or a simple stream of our own internal creativity and eloquence? There has been much study on both sides of these issues.

In my understanding, dreams are the gateway of our spiritual existence. They teach us about our intuitions on a level we have yet to realize. Sometimes they are a pointed and eloquent doorway into teachings from our spiritual guides. There are also messages from the physical plane of existence—such as visitations from a departed relative or close friend—and there are spiritual interpretations or lessons to be learned. This is where most of your beautiful spiritually-based movies, books, and inspirational artwork stems from.

In this plane, we can see where our life is and where it is heading. I will share a recurring dream I had as a youth. Imagine a troubled 20-something, one who had been through a great deal of interpersonal trauma and loss, who had always thought of the greater good and prayed only for proper intention of communication and understanding. My first dream that spelled out the hope of humanity was of a castle on a hill, I termed it as the castle on the hill where the angels come to cry. It was a vibrant yet daunting sight. It was set upon a cliff overlooking the infinite plane. In our realm, we could compare this to the ocean.

On many separate occasions, both in the dream and visionary states, I have been led through this castle, to see its various wondrous and ornate beauties, to speak with and learn from the angels and ascended masters of our history books. They talked to me of their various journeys, goals, and ideals for humankind. They handed me their hope, love, compassion, and desire for purity of the human spirit. This vision and the sequence of these dreams, prayers, and meditations are the spiritual foundation of this book and the many more to come.

Truth be told, the basis of our spiritual core of understanding is awakened in our dream state. We can walk different paths, communicate with others both here and passed, learn valuable lessons from our spiritual guides, and for a moment experience absolute freedom of consciousness. To let the mind wander!

In my youth, I had many vivid dreams. As I grew into adulthood, I was made aware of their enlightenment process. The troubled youth in me put away their lessons and teachings. I tried with all my might to leave behind my natural and divine gifts of love, understanding, and interpretation. The prophetic, spiritual words of universal source flowed through me, yet still I put my proverbial head in the sand due to a continued course of traumatic events.

For many years I stopped writing, reading, or letting my energetic higher-powered source guide my walk in life. This was exactly what I needed to do for the onset of healing. It led me to a path of brutal personal realizations, the perfect plan for my soul growth. I met and was guided by many amazing healers and spiritual guidance counselors on my path. As the saying goes, when the student is ready, the master will appear. I was always ready and have been blessed with many wonderful teachers, experiences, and events in those trying times of personal understanding.

Within the last few years, I have come to the realization that it is by visualizing and realizing our perception of dreams we set ourselves on a course of personal enlightenment, a pathway to our own divine course of communication and education. Letting your energy expand and encompass the lessons of your dreams is no small feat. It takes determination, levels of personal empathy and care, an understanding relationship with your inner divinity, and an aptitude to follow that voice of higher self in your everyday routines.

Think of it, some decisions we make we know will be regrettable actions. The process of awakening our understanding of the dream state helps us to alleviate the necessity to behave in toxic or misbegotten behaviors. We can communicate with true intent rather than fixate on the frustration of not being heard or understood. We begin to act out of love and acceptance of all things when we align within our own internal makeup. In this way, we balance out frustration with our new-found element of self-understanding.

The personal understanding and compassion for your inner and outer feelings is where the freedom of the dream state evolves. This allows us to concentrate on the patterns of opening to our greatest good. Our greatest good is a fundamental aspect of living in self-awareness. By balancing the energies associated in the dream state, we open our minds to a whole new realm of hope, possibility, communication, and enlightenment.

This is just the beginning, though. We are multidimensional beings, and by understanding our dreams, we are simply scratching the surface of our existence. With the amazing and awe-inspiring understanding of dreams. We are ready to embark on the next phase of our path to divine communication within the infinite loop. We are ready to explore our conscious visions to build on our new-found aspect of self-awareness.

Chapter 2 Visions

(Understanding your personal enlightenment)

What exactly is a vision? Is there a difference between a vision and a dream? How do we start having visions, and where do they come from? Having a background in counseling, I love open-ended questions. Asking ourselves these questions will teach us how to understand the highest elements of our individual spirituality and balance. These are common questions we can answer through the process of natural equation. In the dream state, we are sleeping, interpreting our inner directions of the natural mind. A vision, however, is something extremely different. Visions happen in the conscious state. That is the first unique distinction. We can lead our mind into our visionary state in a variety of ways.

Many have come to awareness of visions by alerting themselves to elements of nature. A movement, a shifting, a natural yet not before noticed evolvement of energy or awareness. Some people see lights or abstractions of visible shadows or shapes. Others hear songs in words that they do not recognize or understand. These are all viable courses that enrich our vibrational awareness. To know where you are and what it is that you are seeing, hearing, or interpreting is imperative. This is not only a part of our three-dimensional reality, but we have now gained a foothold into a fourth or even fifth dimension of our human nature and conscious thought process.

Have you ever seen shapes in clouds or noticed a word or faces in a natural structure such as a leaf, flower, or ripple in the water? These are the onset of spiritual visions. It is a predestined course of illumination and awareness. We shall take this philosophy and run with it, as there are many lessons to learn from the onset of spiritually guided visions.

Many mysticisms teach us how to engage our visionary abilities by using simple tools. These tools date back to the dawn of human history. In many North American Native cultures, there were deep states of prayer, meditation, and even the onset of depriving the body of natural resources such as food or water. In other cultures around the globe, there were divining pools such as stone basins of water representing the water of life, candle-lit structures of prayer and meditation, or even mirrors made from various ornate stones. The prophet Nostradamus used an obsidian mirror wrapped in copper to illuminate his visions. Black Elk used the prayer state to guide his inner reality. Monks, priests, even the Pope and the Dalai Lama use this same point of awareness to guide and understand their visions in an everyday occurrence. We can, too.

Every foundational belief system on our beautiful planet earth teaches one supreme thing: to be in a constant state of prayer and meditation. This is where we can touch our divinity and illuminate or understand our spiritually guided visions. We as the people we are can initiate visions wherever we go and whenever we want. All we have to do is open that doorway to our own interpretation of divine consciousness.

In this second building block of our communication with inter dimensional divinity, there has been selected a few pieces of poetry out of the Study journals to help define, activate, and engage the process of visionary enlightenment. Please enjoy as it is an honor to place these in your hands!

Visions Artistic Impressions

1. 12/8/19 - Tet - A candle moves this forward

2. 6/13/20 - Dalet - A gaze into the distance

3. 3/16/20 - Gimel - Now look at all the beauty

4. 6/7/20 - Gimel - The beauty of a mystic

5. 12/11/19 - Zayin - The soul is never empty

6. 12/11/19 - Vav - Chasing down this freedom

7. 6/3/20 - Bet - Where is it we are going

8. 6/14/20 - Gimel - Today upon the sunrise

9. 2/13/20 - Bet - The color blue, the color green

10. 4/11/20 - Bet - To sit within a castle

A candle moves this forward,
so long about a dream.
For visions of this empath,
has brought the heart to scream.

In terror of a triumph,
on the breaking of a mirror.
We drop upon the pages,
a silent softened tear.

With duty moving onward,
upon another day.
We sit on earth-toned structure,
of what we have to say.

The passions of our nature,
on the purity of heart.
Will find a new translation,
of the love we must impart.

12/8/19
Tet

A gaze into the distance,
of sight upon the sphere.
Through eyes of crystal candles,
which tell us not to fear.

There's yet another doorway,
to the staircase of the stars.
Somewhere upon infinity,
are the pyramids of Mars.

The mountaintops are dancing,
upon this distant state.
A hopeful heart is warming,
to this we must relate.

A series or a saga,
of our mini epic time.
Will grant us all due diligence,
to immerse ourselves in rhyme.

6/13/20
Dalet

Now look at all the beauty,
in the process of this sight.
To feel it has purpose,
in the drawing of this right.

Within a wooden hallway,
at the corner of the mind.
We take a step of faith,
to see what we will find.

Encouraged by decisiveness,
now turn at once to see.
The magic of emotion,
and where it's built for thee.

With statues bold and blazoned,
a pool inside this space.
Now open up the mindset,
to give this dream a taste.

3/16/20
Gimel

The beauty of a mystic,
alone within their thought.
A process to awareness,
is all they've truly sought.

A simple golden visage,
of a castle on a hill.
The rooms go on forever,
for infinity they will.

And now of just vibration,
this universe of time.
The power of a spectrum,
encompassed by a rhyme.

Explain the dreams in order,
as someday we will see.
The progress we are making,
within this mystery.

6/7/20
Gimel

The soul is never empty,
this process never mine.
This place is thought and meaning,
a sentiment of time.

Adrift on light and shadow,
we search the inner well.
For beings and for balance,
we seek within our cell.

A current lack of element,
plagues upon the thought.
A system of security,
which we have surely sought.

So wipe away the ashes,
which cry for crystal tears.
And build the true-born wisdom,
with smoke and dragons' fears.

12/11/19
Zayin

Chasing down this freedom,
as if it were a bird.
Passing through a passage,
upon the written word.

We sound about a sequence,
within a distant time.
Where all is just security,
of rhythm and of rhyme.

There is no need for heartache,
for worry or regret.
We all find bright festivities,
in what we've termed as yet.

So slide us in the system,
of the passions call of dreams.
And romance us with the wisdoms,
upon these sacred scenes.

12/11/19
Vav

Where is it we are going,
and what is that we should know?
A verb is used as tenses,
for these places we will go.

We're grifting on the scenery,
with a prayer for only chance.
To move forever forward,
in the music of our dance.

A knight comes here on horseback,
after telling us his toil.
We gander at the moonrise,
far above the earthen soil.

To speak about compassion,
where it meets us on this day.
Then take the time for cleansing,
yes, in each and every way.

6/3/20
Bet

Today upon the sunrise,
We touched the face of love.
In sweet poetic gratitude,
a gift from God above.

We rode upon a whisper,
and danced within a dream.
To see the ounce of beauty,
portrayed inside the scene.

When time gives way for wishes,
in this element called life.
And prayers turn into products,
which quell our bitter strife.

When we are drawn to discourse,
for the betterment of all.
We then may find the message,
in the passion of our call.

4/14/20
Gimel

The color blue,
the color green.
A glint of light,
within the scene.

A textured hue,
a poignant dream.
A draft of vision,
it would seem.

An epic tale,
or so we're told.
May have our time,
as we grow old.

As wind to sail,
or gifts we've sold.
Upon this sight,
we now behold.

2/13/20
Bet

To sit within a castle,
we've built upon our dreams.
With gratitude and empathy,
now surveying its scenes.

The lights they dance around us,
they flicker as in flame.
The songbirds bring their bounty,
and their beauty is the same.

A paradise unquestioned,
inside the open mind.
A route to be discovered,
through the paradox we find.

While crystal clear the vision,
of days so long ago.
Now stew upon simplicity,
of what we've yet to know.

4/11/20
Bet

When we think we are having a vision, how do we tend to interpret it? Using your own intuitive knowledge is always the best course. Many people will tell you it has to be this way or that way. This limits us to a black-and-white concept from another person's perspective. As we become aware of our spiritual understanding and awareness, this is exactly what we should shy away from. This is your vision, your guidance. Your vision is for you.

There are no black-and-white perspectives on spiritual visions. There are, in fact, myriads of color. These are teachings given only to us by our ancestors and guides. They are thoughts and theories that cannot be interpreted by a closed mind. They, however, can and should be discussed as topics of awareness in conversations we have on a daily basis. Use open and intimate communication in these exchanges. Let your friends and loved ones give their opinions about your interpretation. Be ready to hear their thoughts and quite possibly their visions as well. At this point, we are opening a channel of divine interpretation. This is how we begin to evolve into our higher states of conscious awareness.

What we are currently laying out before us is a roadmap to a greater understanding. An understanding that will free the limitations we put on ourselves. Many people have come up with the saying that we need to think outside of the box. I am asking, "Why is there even a box?" We are beings of spirituality through consciousness. We are set on this path of existence to accumulate understanding, awareness, and experience the aspect of being human. There are no constraints to pure consciousness. There is no box for dreams and visions. We must learn to interpret our own understanding to become one within the beauty and balance of the universal energy field.

Sometimes we have to slow down our mind to allow our thoughts to catch up. This is why we dream. This is why we are guided to see visions of beauty and balance. These are the building blocks that format our awareness. When we allow our own intuition to guide us, we are opening ourselves to faith in our higher selves. Our higher selves will always lead us on the perfect path for us and allow us to freely show love to all others we encounter.

What lies inside our dreams and visions is guidance and awareness. This is laid out for us by the consciousness of our creation. The energy field that frees us and our experience to begin its course of communication with the divine. This is where we begin our understanding of the aspects of intuition and knowledge of the greater good. It is here where we find the hopeful dreams of our true spirit and heal the chaotic echoes of our daily existence.

When we can discuss our interpretation of our dreams and visions, we begin to meet the guiding elements of our true spiritual path. We are met by both guidance counselors in the physical realm, spirit guides in our metaphysical mind, ascended masters, and, yes, even the angelic figures who guide and guard the beauty of our divine creation.

We are now entering a pathway to the creative identity of divine spirituality. Through understanding our dreams and interpreting our visions, we open the mind to a whole new world of beauty and balance. We start to see the gifts of our own personal divinity and grace. We have been met by many teachers and have started to see the whole of universal connectedness.

This is where we start our path. We are on a trail to the beautiful and wondrous places of our infinite surroundings. Dimensions of purity, solace, and peace are opening up to us on a moment-by-moment basis. Through these first small steps, we have gained an understanding of the spiritual realm. Now we are ready to open our mind and our emotions to interpret the divine energies guiding us on the spiritual level of this existence. We are ready to start chatting with our angels.

Chapter 3 Angels
(Conversations and communication; yours, mine and ours)

When we first hear the word "angel" or "angelic," what comes to mind? Right off the bat, we are using our visionary abilities as we have a picture or idea in our head. Angels walk among us constantly. They are everywhere and inside of everything we witness and interpret. It is up to us to hear them and understand their individual and divine teachings.

There are many philosophies that define angelic beings. The Bible speaks of the many divine armies of angels that protect and defend the gates of Heaven and God's grace and mercy. There are also Sumerian and Egyptian teachings, which define seven archangels and their unique aptitudes of enlightenment. The Essene gospels state that both the Heavenly Father and Earthly Mother have seven respective angelic forces that embody their individual teachings. So, which is true? The answer is yes.

The more angels we have around us, the better we learn to communicate. We can study all of them in different areas of research in our spiritual path. Angels are beings, much like you and I. They have personalities, emotions, understanding, and guidance from the above. Whether we are talking about guiding natural forces, such as the Essene Angel of the Peace, or learning about the teachings of Gabriel and Michael from the Biblical, Sumerian, and Egyptian teachings, angelic understandings are imperative to the growth of our personal enlightenment and divine communication process.

There are many other guiding esoteric, dimensional, and cosmic beings, still angels are the first and foremost of our spirit guides as they have the purest and most direct channel to universal source. There are also human guides, your individual ancestors or departed relatives, ascended masters who have internalized the aspects of divinity while they walked their path on Earth, and, of course, a vast array of other cosmic and interplanetary life-forms and entities such as fairies, reptilians, or dragons.

This is where our foundational element of dreams and visions becomes vital to our communication process. Through these understandings we can start having conversations with these

40

Angelic, spiritual and dimensional entities. We can become more aware of what they are saying to us without putting our conscious thought patterns in the way. When we see something beautiful, we can understand the beauty and know it was placed upon our path as a guiding light in our circumstantial environment. Much more, we can start having conversations with the energies that we are beginning to see, feel, and interpret.

Angels are humble and compassionate beings; they are servants of our Creator's guidance and council. They have deep personal reverence for universal blessings and live in the autonomy of their own individuality. They have been gifted many different names by the Creator for their distinct personality traits; therefore, it is less imperative to know their individual names, yet rather, to internalize their spiritual guidance and teachings.

This communication is the first and fundamental aspect of living in higher-self guidance and awareness. Angelic beings talk to us, and it is with the universal language that we get to interpret what they are saying. They desire for all of us to know and illuminate our personal greatest good. What are we working on in this lifetime, and how can they help? With our understanding, we can hear their voices, see their faces, listen to their songs, and walk hand in hand within their gifted guidance of love, hope, promise, and reverence for the passion of our Creator.

Starting with the internalization of the dream state and the opening of our basic intuitions of visionary potential, we are now standing in an ever-expanding interpretation of angelic and divine guidance. Here are a few pieces of poetry from the Study journals, which were channeled for the illumination process of the angelic and divine realms of communication. Please enjoy them with my kindest regards and warmest blessings.

Angels Artistic Impressions

1. On the greenish hue of angels - 6/14/20 - Dalet

2. And here the light is shining - 3/16/20 - Bet

3. To speak of only bounty - 11/18/20 - Gimel

4. A parable of resource - 5/24/20 - Dalet

5. In tragedies of comfort - 1/27/20 - Dalet

6. To see you on a candle - 6/7/20 - Bet

7. To hear the call of angels - 5/24/20 - Gimel

8. A crazy counterbalance - 1/27/20 - Gimel

9. The angels of our aura - 2/9/20 - Gimel

10. An angel in this vision - 6/1/20 - Bet

On the greenish hue of angels,
or the beauty of a sight.
We speak about our vision,
and encompass inner light.

The breaking down to basics,
in the proverb of our time.
Through ancient books of knowledge,
and words of written rhyme.

We set ourselves to journey,
in conquest of our dreams.
Yet do we stop to question,
just what our vision means?

Complete within the color,
of the places we will go.
We dive to newfound depths,
of the knowledge we must know.

6/14/20
Dalet

And here the light is shining,
cascading down like rain.
Removing just the darkness,
or the likeness of disdain.

With pure poetic purpose,
its prose is only truth.
And comes this way in stages,
from the fountains of our youth.

A well with wish for wisdom,
or a penny for your thought.
To sit upon the sequence,
of just the sight you've sought.

We've come with thirst for fire,
from the passion of a dream.
With the angels at our altar,
we embrace the perfect scene.

3/16/20
Bet

To speak of only bounty,
a brilliant brand of fate.
Befalling words of wisdom,
for those who will relate.

We meditate on silence,
an inner verse because.
Within that deft vibration,
is all that ever was.

Transparent hidden echoes,
are angels in the sky.
They speak to us in secret,
preparing us to fly.

Believe on only blessings,
for dear or faint of heart.
There are some structured truths,
which they've come to impart.

11/18/20
Gimel

A parable of resource,
comes streaming through the light.
To teach us of transcendence,
the purpose of our plight.

In colors of creation,
from black to white as snow.
We try to learn the lessons,
the teachings each must know.

To find for us the future,
of hope we all can share.
To pine about the promise,
of the one we all must care.

So take me to Creator,
oh, angels of my dreams.
To show us true the passion,
We sense within these scenes.

5/24/20
Dalet

In tragedies of comfort,
made from murals of a dream.
We knock a distant doorway,
where the angels come to scream.

Somewhere inside the sanctity,
we structure what we seek.
When not bespawned by ego,
in prayers of kind and meek.

As gentle as a daydream,
and soft as starlit night.
We build our infrastructure,
on the series of this sight.

Elude with me to echoes,
fixing fractures of our mind.
Ride sheltered on this pathway,
to see what we shall find.

1/27/20
Dalet

To see you on a candle,
to sense you in a dream.
To survey all the scenery,
within this sacred scene.

Now sit upon a storm cloud,
awaiting skies of blue.
And as the day approaches,
I'm praying now for you.

Protected by the dragon,
with miracles inside.
We're shown the path of angels,
and in us they confide.

To walk up to their mountain,
to hear their hopeful prayer.
To behold light and darkness,
and then with you we'll share.

6/7/20
Bet

To hear the call of angels,
to go where eagles dare.
To point upon the caption,
of what we've come to share.

Now sit in sublimation,
of only thought or deed.
To write about the wisdom,
of just our truest need.

Following our spirit,
upon this path of gold.
Walking in the footsteps,
to God we're surely told.

A brilliant ray of crystal,
emblazoned by a flame,
Captures current concept,
to give this path a name.

5/24/20
Gimel

A crazy counterbalance,
it rides on waves of winds.
To structure sacred scenery,
Yes, through our heart it swims.

The master stone remembered,
as clearly as the sky.
With quartz of crystal theory,
we see their reasons why.

The mind may have a tantrum,
the heart may skip a beat.
Yet touching is our tenderness,
inside this fire's heat.

The angels of our passions,
speak kindness to this fate.
Please let us once deliver,
their message to relate.

1/27/20
Gimel

The angels of our aura,
the building of their stage.
The process of our passion,
has turned another page.

In times of tempting silence,
to burn the candles light.
We wax about foundation,
and wane what's true and right.

To balance human ego,
on the sphere within this space.
We trust inside the concept,
of pure and quaint embrace.

To knock upon the doorway,
in the hallway of our dreams.
And find now just the future,
in the structure of those scenes.

2/9/20
Gimel

An angel in this vision,
foundation in the hand.
The colors of concordance,
to purveyance of the plan.

Our fate upon the future,
be it want or wish or will.
Is divine-inspired calling,
now to climb atop this hill.

We sit inside a capsule,
born of beauty, wrapped in love.
To word the ways of wisdom,
for our counterparts above.

To someday ride the lightning,
in their effervescent sky.
And build our wings from wishes,
as upon these sights we fly.

6/1/20
Bet

Angels have come to me at many points in my life. They have led me through times of heartache and celebrated with me in times of joy and triumph. They can and will with you as well. For the compilation of this work, I was pointed in a direction, handed a format to awareness, and given the words to put on each page. I am a simple poet. My true gift is interpretation and understanding of the divine, and I have been led to put that gift in print and share it with you. I am so grateful and filled with hope that you are reading this interpretation of divine communication and guidance. To me that means you are ready to understand and take care of yourself. Possibly for the first time in your life.

Angels, fairies, dragons, and any other creatures both real and imagined are with us all. They help us divine our own elements of understanding. They teach us concepts that we may not conceive of in our limited human comprehension. They travel with us, walk with us, and guide us in so many ways.

Many people have stated that we each have two angels on our shoulders, whispering in our ears, one good and one bad. That we choose who we listen to and take direction from. While this is true, it is also true that the universe is not created from a black-and-white perspective. It was created from life-force energy inside a myriad of colors and understanding.

What we are embarking on currently is a quest to develop our senses. We are here to illuminate our awareness. To define and drive our conscious state to the next phase of our existence. It is by understanding the lessons put out for us here, in this plane, that we transcend properly into the next layers of dimensional consciousness.

Angels are here to show us these interpretations. I suggest talking to them without preconceived notions of how they might react. They speak fluently and eloquently. Write it down. It is usually a telepathic communication sent to us as an emotion, yet I have been both touched and heard voices in song, this is much more of an understanding. Sometimes you will have no idea what you are writing, yet the teachings will be illuminated when you read your own channeled messages from the center of this angelic source.

The same goes for other spiritual beings. I work with angels constantly, and they love to have their words written. Dragons, on the other hand, prefer to be talked with, understood, and go on missions for you. Names while not extremely important to an angel are to a dragon. Ask and you shall receive. Fairies, however, are the loving energies of Earthborn elements. They are here to teach us how to interact within our natural world. To give it blessings and treat it with the beauty and balance each one of us deserves to be treated with. We can see all of this in reverence or by communicating in the universal language. At this point, the important part is to use your dreams and visions to guide your spiritual self to this spot of inner divinity.

The pathway of communication within your own personal inter dimensional divinity is intuitive. What we are defining is a course to engage the literal translation. We understand that our dreams are an imperative art form to our higher learning, that by opening our visionary abilities, we set ourselves en route to understand the great divine, and now we can work with our angels and guides to find counsel in where we are going and how to live within the love and hope of our unique spiritual guidance and awareness.

Where is it that we go from here, what languages should we speak, what should we use in our personal art forms of spirituality to explore a deeper and more intuitive understanding? These answers are why I was urged to write this book. It is in the next stage of our spiritual enlightenment process where we explore the foundation note of our universal language: the driving force of creation is in the communication and understanding of passion.

Chapter 4 Passion
(The driving force of creation)

What is passion other than a driving force? It comes innately in each one of us, and we use it to fuel our dreams, desires, and goals. The universe, the angels, and the Creator are the same way. They communicate to us in passionate endeavors within our daily routines. Passion is the first note in the chord structure of the language of universal understanding, and this is set as the fourth layer on our path because we have just started talking to these divine beings. Now we are ready to speak the first layer of their universal language. Everything that is created begins as a passionate endeavor. With this insight, we set forward on our journey in learning the building blocks of communication in our personal inter dimensional divinity.

When Spirit compelled me to start this work, their passion for its creation was so evident that we could not contain our interpretations and life lessons without an avenue to describe their capacities for compassion, love, hope, and understanding. My life has taken a great deal of tragic and wonderful twists and turns. I had the opportunity to work in many various and beautiful capacities at the grassroots level of our social makeup. When I was a boy, I had an aptitude and passion for learning about history, religion, art, and culture.

Classic education was not nearly as important to me as the desire for enlightenment in spiritual thoughts and theories. I wondered how a society built upon art, culture, faith, and diversity could treat each other with misjudgment, condemnation, or lack of empathy. A desire developed to treat each part of our existence with love, peace, communication, and understanding. This afforded the opportunity to walk in inspired higher-self guidance. Being a simple, philosophical poet has been no easy feat. There has always been more desire for truth, passion, and romance than many people could handle. I recall writing books of poetry for multiple people, handing it to them, and saying, "Here, this is yours." The words were a gift to me so they should be regifted in their intended direction.

The first book I intended on writing for publication was

going to be a plea for artisans to fully engage in their greatest gifts. One of my early pieces is titled "A Call to Arts." It is a beautiful epic poem of how creation happened from the artisans' standpoint. I still have this piece in "the Study" and review it quite often. This book is affixed in the embers of my fire and will be the fifth book in The Series of Divine Alchemy. We are all artists by nature. Whether you are a doctor, architect, photographer, scientist, whatever your trade or passion is, you are on the road to discovery in your chosen pathway of enlightenment.

Within the last few years, there has been a great deal of personal transformation. There has been the joy of completing some life goals and restarting some old ones. The poems and spiritually-balanced formats of awareness in this book are all interpreted in what I have termed "The Study Project." Over 90% of the pieces in this book were channeled inside this sacred space, and all of the formats were handed down after its conception. This is my passion: to keep an open mind over where our spirit is leading us to on a daily basis while having a place that prompts the awareness of feeling grounded and complete.

Passion is the driving force of any creation. Each element of our design was gifted through passionate works. Inside of passion is the comprehension that guides us as each new day arises. Within it, we are greeted with hope on the smiling faces of our loved ones. We see the passion and creativity of our Creator when we look at the natural elements around us. Gaze at the sky, the rocks, the trees, the water, sand, anything you find beautiful. Interpret its energy. What is it saying to you? You know when a bird or a dog is trying to tell you something. You can literally hear an animal's voice as it looks at you. The elemental forces of nature communicate in the same way and manner. Try to listen and hold the healing balance of that beautiful communication.

Believe in yourself as a passionate creator using your gifts and skills. We communicate our hope and love by freely flowing within our passionate selves. How much greater will this world be when we truly attempt to live in our personal elements of hope, duty to others, and compassion for all? It is here on our journey through the driving force of creation that I would love to share some excerpts from the study journals. Please enjoy and formulate your own thoughts and theories. We are all waiting to hear them.

Passion Artistic Impressions

1. An arduous endeavor - 2/6/20 - Dalet

2. Just thinking now of chocolate - 2/27/20 - Bet

3. Can we climb this mountain - 4/15/20 - Zayin

4. A sphere of sacred roses - 1/21/20 - Gimel

5. A precipice or pendulum - 1/20/20 - Bet

6. This passion is for purity - 1/28/20 - Bet

7. A dollar found so frequent - 10/19/20 - Bet

8. Exploding now with passion - 1/15/20 - Hay

9. Another view of roses - 3/21/20 - Dalet

10. So draw within the discourse - 1/18/20 - Bet

An arduous endeavor,
takes patience, plan, and time.
The love about forever,
stands riddled in this rhyme.

With Alpha and Omega,
there is no in between.
To gauge a concrete concourse,
within a vaulted dream.

So slipping ever forward,
on the energy of light.
In the quartz of passion's power,
on the romance of the night.

The glitter glistens greatly,
from inside the heart of mind.
As the pages turn so silent,
to see what we may find.

2/6/20
Dalet

Just thinking now of chocolate,
of ration truth be told.
As simple as the starlight,
in tales never told.

So draw into the picture,
just another right of way.
In dreams of light becoming,
on the element of day.

A passion with a purpose,
stands strong upon our mind.
We gift the heart to vision,
to see what God may find.

We're trusting now in wisdom,
no catch within the clause.
On romances of passion,
to find the perfect pause.

2/27/20
Bet

Can we climb this mountain,
could we crest that hill?
May we find the passion,
of this romance to instill?

Move forever forward,
onward to your dream.
Finally find the answer,
on the universal stream.

Conscious inner echoes,
come to meet our gaze.
Now give them understanding,
to clear away the haze.

Draw close to this doorstep,
to believe in only truth.
While we still have posterity,
to channel love and youth.

4/15/20
Zayin

A sphere of sacred roses,
brought romance once this way.
A bright and boundless moment,
on the memory of that day.

In the tragedy of triumph,
or impassioned states of dreams.
We shelter in security,
to what this moment means.

We're blessed with only beauty,
in the core of our romance.
Unbridled is this passion,
when given only chance.

On points upon our clarity,
about this sacred sphere.
We're grateful for protection,
to alleviate all fear.

1/21/20
Gimel

A precipice or pendulum,
be it upside down.
A kindness of conspiracy,
on a smile or a frown.

A vision of the limelight,
at once so far away.
Has brought us to this moment,
upon this very day.

Inside the heart is passion,
for balancing of hope.
A term to pay it forward,
to teach it how to cope.

With ever-present daydreams,
inside these drops of dew.
In the angels of our aura,
We're thinking now of you.

1/20/20
Bet

This passion is for purity,
yet discord lies within.
We see it strike to conflict,
the egregiousness of sin.

Now sit in light becoming,
here praying for romance.
In gifts of the Creator,
to laugh and play and dance.

The devil at our doorstep,
still knocks to come inside.
To buy away this vision,
and take what we have tried.

Salute internal instinct,
in the process of this course.
To build a brilliant future,
in the sounding of the source.

1/28/20
Bet

A dollar found so frequent,
in waves upon the sand.
Brings platforms of subsistence,
to what is now at hand.

Immersed by wave-like structure,
a chorus of our dreams.
The center of our shelter,
is wrought with ways and means.

So open your horizon,
to greet the newfound day.
And see within reflection,
the path of one true way.

This energetic echo,
reverberates the sight.
As we are drawn to discourse,
of what we'll find tonight.

10/19/20
Bet

Exploding now with passion,
into another sight.
Upon a deft discussion,
of what is good and right.

Now send upon a heartbeat,
the molecule of time.
And build within foundation,
the rhythm of its rhyme.

Sit down upon the sunrise,
in the shelter of your sky.
Fix the fractured feeling,
which bore the question why.

Ego is an insult,
too creator to be true.
As fire takes this fury,
and restores the heart to you.

1/15/20
Hay

Another view of roses,
on the dawning of the day.
Upon a softened echo,
of the proper words to say.

Now see the bunnies balance,
on the beam of just their life.
Forgetting all their toils,
to eliminate their strife.

In chaos there's confusion,
of everything we do.
In peace we have posterity,
to let ourselves be true.

And thus we pen these pages,
from the quantum of our mind.
To draft within this diction,
what wisdoms we may find.

3/21/20
Dalet

So draw within the discourse,
of you and just your God.
Bring yourself to basics,
of prayer and passions nod.

Disciple simple praises,
in the gratitude you give.
On the moments of your heartache,
just find a way to live.

We sit in certain echo,
just thinking rays of thought.
Emboldened by this amplitude,
to seek the sights we've sought.

In what it is this daydream,
upon our sacred sphere.
To see inside forever,
in the structure of right here.

1/18/20
Bet

Passion is at the core of our emotional and spiritual beings. It is the first emotion that begins our understanding or connection to universal blessings. A friend once told me that the first time they felt truly connected, to the universe, was at the moment they first held their newborn. I agreed and said, "Yes, yet when was your baby created, that was a passionate endeavor."

Communicating in passion manifests itself constantly in our daily lives. If you are angry, upset, or feeling love, romance, expressing empathy or judgment, be aware that passion is at the root of these emotional reactions. It is something we feel deep inside. It is the very core of our existence and a tool to understand as we travel further down our spiritual path.

In every flow of energy, the heartbeat of that focal point is a passionate endeavor. The properties of magnetic impulse, gravity, push, and pull are all understood by engaging the passion within the response. We could now be talking about balancing chakras or feeding a loved one dinner. Passion flows from the universe. When we feel attracted by certain people, places, or ideals that is a direct result of the passion we feel for their intuition and understanding. It is a balance of energy from one to another. This is the first and primary of our elemental understandings. Without passion, there could be no emotion, ideology, self-determination, or aspects of free will.

We see passion in every encounter we have, with either humans or the natural world. Like that one time you wanted to make a point, couldn't formulate the accurate words, then got frustrated or the flower which grew out of the tiny crack in the concrete you passed on the way to work. These are all parables of passion in our everyday life.

So how do we employ passion? How do we use it to garner and maintain our greatest good? At first, we notice it. We can look at all the elements of passion which permeate our daily lives. Notice the emotion associated with it. Find the underlying factor in the dawning of the certain dream which is being fulfilled right in front of you, and, of course, learn to speak the universal language: gratitude!

We haven't gotten to the gratitude chapter yet. Still when we spoke of angels in the last chapter they are full of reverence and respect. They speak from the elements of passion, gratitude and love. The foundation of their 1, 3, 5 major chord structure is the emotion of passion. Passion, gratitude, and love are those building blocks to attain overall vibrational awareness communication with our points of inner and outer divinity, and the individual essence of understanding universal source codes. Each perception will ebb and flow through us at different intervals to balance our highest and best sense of awareness into a combined state of universal consciousness.

We can hear these emotions in audible tones. Many hear ringing or whistling when they are channeling messages from their angels and spirit guides. Some feel vibrations, and they might get goosebumps or shivers when this communication is happening. The way to understand what they are saying is to reach out in emotional empathy. Begin to understand the ringing like you might understand that water moves through the ground or flows within a tree. That way we are setting ourselves to become one within universal interpretation and communication.

Through passion, all creation flows. There are many diverse belief systems on how creation happened—from Biblical teachings to the Big Bang theory, and everything in between. Even if all of them happened, passion was and still remains the driving force behind it. Our universe, the holy enlightened beings, our masters of creation and individuality all employ the truest aspects of passion, and so can we.

Once we start opening our lives to the upper vibrations of dimensional transference, we ebb and flow into different aspects of reason and understanding. The original building blocks of this awareness were laid out in the first three chapters. We have understood the dream state, began looking into our visionary abilities, then associated the guidance and protection of our angels. Now with the understanding that passion is the driving force of creation and the first of the universal languages, we open the door to a whole new realm of possibility and enlightenment.

So what do we do with this knowledge? Where do we go with our passionate responses and understanding? How do we take the fire from the depth of our very awareness and use it to do its best and purest work? For this, there can be only one answer: We have to reach deep down into the elemental core of our being, use our wealth of knowledge, access the spiritual center of our understanding, and open those conversations with our angels, guides, and Creator. With humility and reverence, we have internalized the first language of universal source. We realize that communication with everything is not only possible, it is truly a constant part of our human existence. Once we can talk, it's time to communicate. Now, we open up and pray.

Chapter 5 Prayers
(the process of knowing what to ask for and how to ask)

What is a prayer? How do we open up a conversation with the divine beings surrounding us? How do we put our minds in a place of passion, gratitude, and love, that perfectly balanced spot where we can converse with spirit without bringing our wills and egos? After all, these are very prolific human attributes. We have already talked about this answer a few times; It is to always come from a point of reverence for spirit, respect of self and others, humility that we are each autonomous beings, and, of course, joy for the natural settings we get to be a part of in our daily routines.

Somewhere deep inside, we realize that when talking to angels or our Creator, communication is very different than when we are conversing with friends or relatives. Using passion as the first of our universal languages, we begin to internalize the contrast of how we can achieve an emotional understanding that all prayers are not only heard yet answered within the elements of universal source.

To pray is not only to ask the Creator's guidance or to receive certain things. It is very much an open, passionate conversation where we can show our gratitude for the blessings we are gifted on our path. We can express our joy and reverence or interject thought and theory for all of the divine beauty we experience. Thank the universe when it has provided you food, family, friends, impassioned moments, and loved ones on your path. These are the faithful, joyous graces of our individual divine spirit.

It may be that we, as humans, are all cracked and broken in some ways. Here in the prayer state is where we can change that aspect of ourselves. Let it grow into the healing rays of hope and guidance from our Creator. This is a great deal of what we pray for, and these requests are always answered innately, just by our intention of the question. Through asking for healing, we are receiving divine healing. The Creator will guide and bless us simply by opening this conversation. We are all bodies of light and guidance set upon our path to work on achieving our life goals. The Creator, pure angelic beings, and the universe itself all wish to aid us on our course of personal enlightenment. All we have to do is ask.

Many different religious and metaphysical teachings stand in unison on the aspects of prayer. They all state that we can ask for anything we choose in any area of our lives, as long as we do so on a continuing basis from a humble and meek perspective. This is why we are taught to bow, kneel, or hold our hands in a certain manner to show reverence, respect, or gratitude, and show the creator our own unique understanding of divine grace and mercy.

When we approach the Creator from the truly meek and humble aspects of human existence, some wonderful and beautiful things happen in our lives. We begin to treat each part of our lives with that same reverence, respect, and divinity. We associate, in our minds, the true nature of our reality being as gifted and blessed to us by our Creator. We see the sky as spiritual, the earth as a spiritual being, we notice the innate spirituality and creative blessings in everything and everyone we see or connect with on our path.

These blessings are revealed to us on a moment-by-moment basis. When we treat everything as sacred or spiritual, we are walking in unison with our environment. Menial daily tasks seem more enjoyable, and we are free to walk in our greatest good. This is the true nature of our spirit.

Many people across cultures use poetry as a way of showing gratitude to all things and as a reference point for their conversations with the Creator. The following pieces were selected to show the ceremony of life. Please enjoy these prayers. They were written for the world as a whole, and you are an integral part of everything. Yes, I said it; these prayers are for you, for me, for our very existence and the oneness of the universal spirit.

Prayers Artistic Impressions

1. Upon the truest vision - 11/29/19 - Hay

2. So bring us to becoming - 2/9/20 - Bet

3. As Creator grants direction - 12/28/19 - Bet

4. To want for no more hatred - 12-22-19 - Bet

5. Thank you for these blessings - 6/15/20 - ?

6. So bring to us your bitterness - 1/27/20 - Bet

7. A breath for inner structure - 2/6/20 - Gimel

8. To seal up your trauma - 6/5/20 - Bet

9. The caring light of fire - 6/5/20 - Gimel

10. The beauty of becoming - 3/26/20 - Bet

Upon the truest vision,
within this deepest night.
We delve to dive much further,
for this we know is right.

In safety of the silence,
in elements of dreams.
We wage our war of wonder,
to find out what it means.

Benign has become freedom,
so passive yet so pure.
The spot it comes to call,
are those moments we endure.

We're sitting on a precipice,
of once upon a prayer.
And calling to the heavens,
that you could meet us there.

11/29/19
Hay

So bring us to becoming,
inside this learning curve.
Teach of the belonging,
to just the God we serve.

In pure and simple mindsets,
upon another night.
Open up these dreams,
to show us what is right.

Alleviate injustice,
within our breaking heart.
Find inside foundation,
the time to stop and start.

In fire we find freedom,
in passion we sense love.
In romance there's reaction,
yet what now lies above?

2/9/20
Bet

As Creator grants direction,
to a pure and simple man.
He speaks to them of courses,
to illuminate the plan.

As silent as a shadow,
in the sheltered dreams of night.
This process of perception,
sometimes gets lost in sight.

So speak to us our maker,
from the swept wind of the trees.
Buzz us with your brilliance,
through the beauty of the bees.

Grant us just the gratitude,
in kindness of your way.
On the simple undertaking,
of all we do and say.

12/28/19
Bet

To want for no more hatred,
no judgment and no pain.
No deep or dark depression,
which permeates the brain.

We see the brutal sunlight,
the beauty bounce around.
To find this inner palace,
inside the sites we've found.

To travel once to nowhere,
just deep inside the mind.
To feel as an echo,
in a distant left behind.

We pray now for the passion,
for this purity of life.
For the morning sun to find us,
without internal strife.

12/22/19
Bet

Thank you for these blessings,
these building blocks of dreams.
The quaint yet burning echoes,
which teach us of your scenes.

We see them as a shadow,
yet doubt not their intent.
As all must be enlightened,
when they are heaven sent.

Come to me, Creator,
open up my mind.
Turn my fear to mercy,
teach me to be kind.

Now driving down a pathway,
between a want or will.
Show us to the mountain,
and help us climb the hill.

6/15/20
Bet

So bring to us your bitterness,
set it at our feet.
Watch the metamorphosis,
as it becomes complete.

A silent sacred structure,
vibrates upon the hill.
As we succumb to reason,
and gift to God our will.

So near and dear Creator,
the building block of dreams.
Speak to us of passion,
to tell now what it means.

Betrayed has been the boundary,
we saw it coming true.
To ask for nothing more,
then we now grant to you.

1/27/20
Bet

A breath for inner structure,
a foundation to instill.
Bereft of needless nonsense,
or egos of the will.

We sit in light transcription,
on the universe of thought.
And sing into the heavens,
about the sights we've sought.

In balance of this vision,
on the introspective sight.
We gauge the contemplation,
of what is heard as right.

A message to the maker,
a prayer of love and hope.
Created by compassion,
that all will one day cope.

2/6/20
Gimel

To seal up your trauma,
and cast it straight away.
To find the pure vibration,
of each and every day.

Assuage the tastes of bitter,
as sweet becomes the dream.
To build the true foundation,
upon the sacred scene.

We sit here brought by color,
a rainbow we've been told.
The power of a promise,
way back from days of old.

In grains of just compassion,
or knowledge yet to learn.
We pray now for due process,
in this candle that we burn.

6/5/20
Bet

The caring light of fire,
the healing rays of hope.
The countless and concurrent,
many ways we've come to cope.

This passion is belonging,
to the sources of our truth.
The building blocks of wisdom,
on divine forever youth.

Come guide us now, Creator,
in the ways you want of me.
Accept me as I am,
so we can finally see.

That beauty is belonging,
to the presence you create.
And leave a sight of reference,
for our loved ones to relate.

6/5/20
Gimel

The beauty of becoming,
a will that's meant to be.
A level left to open,
inside this mystery.

Protect our inner shelter,
we ask you now, my lord.
We pray for you, Creator,
it's all we can afford.

In gallant human trials,
on the wisdom of what's right.
We build upon the pretense,
of an ever-growing sight.

Now watch the shelters crumble,
of those who can't believe.
And try to teach profoundly,
before we take our leave.

3/26/20
Bet

To pray without cease or end. Prayer is a constant passionately-inspired state that stems from an omnipotent perspective. We are always in communication with our higher self and the Creator of our divine reality. Sometimes it is difficult to grasp the concept of omnipotence or omnipresence, especially from the direction of a single divine force of energy. All energy has a focal point, an origin if you will. The creation of our universe is no different. There is a single point of energetic fluctuation that guides our creative and life-force energies. We can see this focal point in the light energies of every living thing.

The prayer state is a way of communicating with that omnipotent energy. We are letting that energy know of our wants, wishes, and desires. We are communicating our gratitude for the blessings and beauty we have found in the reality it has created for us. We are constantly writing and rewriting universal source codes through our behaviors, actions, and communications with this great I Am.

The teaching I have received on the prayer state is to always come from a point of reverence and respect for every living and elemental thing, as these are the aspects of the great omnipotence. Elemental beings are very much alive. If you look at the process of an atom or molecule, it has a gravitational push or pull to it. Where there is movement, there is life force energy. Where there is life force energy there is the residual aspect of divine omnipotence. We are praying to and through everything that is, was, and ever shall be. That is the origin of universal connectedness.

We all have the power of prayer and can learn to harness it. The more we pray for others the easier it is for our guides, angels, and the Creator to understand we are coming from a place of hope and love. We are using our divine energy to help and heal, rather than sit within our own self-indulgence. We can not only pray for ourselves and the people we know, but also for the Creator, our Earth, and even the universe as a whole.

Any of the traditional or non-traditional prayer states are very applicable to a personal prayer state. For centuries across all cultures, many people have used smoke as a way of lifting prayers to the Creator: There are fires and sage from many Native cultures worldwide, churches use candles and incense, and all cultures use chanting or reverent verbiage to initiate talking to God.

The important thing is to initiate it and use it as a primary point of intention, rather than a secondary format of a haphazard belief system. When we are talking with our Creator, it should always be at the forefront of our mindset. This is where we find guidance to do our greatest good. This is where we find the humanity to treat everything around us with universal love and divine understanding.

Look around at the natural forces within your sight. See the sky, the trees, the mountains, the water, talk to them as if you are talking to a sacred or divine friend. Let them know how much you appreciate them coming to guide you and gift your day with grace and beauty. Speak about the desire to watch them heal and grow as you yourself engage healing and growth. The earth itself could use guidance and healing, just like the rest of us.

When we learn to constantly communicate within our greatest good, we will also begin listening to the answers provided by the spirit of our creation. These conversations are just like the ones we have in our everyday lives. How would we communicate with others if we didn't allow any guidance to flow back to us? How would we know a friend if they weren't allowed to tell us what they were thinking?

For these answers, we should look past our prayers. We can strip away everything that is not in our truest nature. With our feet firm on the ground, we can reach into the universe and begin to hear our greatest calling. We have created balance inside the original natures of our spiritual selves. We have built that foundation within our dreams and visions, then we have accessed the intuitive knowledges of our unique angels and guides. Through the prayer state we have initiated the conversation of our intentions to the universe. Now we are ready for our prayers to be answered, our voices to be heard, and our Creator to speak directly to us. we willfully open up the elemental state of our human nature. We are ready to learn meditation as the next vibrant component in our intentional communication with divinity.

Chapter 6 Meditation

(Creative identity; understanding your inner self to identify within everything)

Beginning a chapter devoted solely to the arts of meditation, tempting to speak to all of our relations at once. We have begun to understand ourselves as an enlightened spiritual being through our dream state and visionary awarenesses. We have opened the door to talking to angels and our personal divine teachers and guides. We have understood passion is the first universal language, and we have initiated our prayer state in a constant conscious contact with the divine. Now we get to unlock the door for relational understanding or interpretive communication, inside of this firm spiritual foundation. It is here we begin an initial awareness which leads us to the higher states of universal consciousness.

The arts of meditation provide a path to understand ourselves, others, and creation as a whole. They, diverse meditations, are a singular life breathing entity. Through engaging meditation, we begin to hear the answers to our prayers and receive divine guidance and counsel. Meditation is the fundamental basis of listening to the energies that are not only inside of us but also surround, embody, and encompass our every thought and action. Where Passion is the first language, meditation is the first element of universal source.

For the beginning meditator, the process may seem foreign, even vague, at first. If you're more advanced, you are already aware of the aspects of your inner and outer energy fields. The process of beginning a meditation is fairly simple, so let's start at the beginning and see where it goes.

Currently, we are on a path of communication between our divine selves and universal source, this is exactly what meditation does. It brings the mind and body together in a grounded state of equanimity. From there, we are free to choose the direction of the free-flowing mind. The process of balancing stress, trauma, and daily chaotic events seem to flow out of our persona as easily as it flowed in. All we have to do is remain calm, remember to breathe, and ground ourselves to the natural states of being one, inside of this universal consciousness.

Many people guide their bodies into states of meditation from external influences. Having studied a bit of psychology, I became aware that runners and swimmers have the quietest minds of those who exercise because there is little outside influence, to the conscious mind, when engaging in those activities. That is also the reason why many people who drive long distances by themselves enjoy a sense of calm or peace behind the wheel. Yet what is the difference between certain exercises, driving, and the meditative arts, and how can we build this simple routine into our daily lives?

There are many diverse types of meditation, so which one is right? Keeping with the logic of this similar question in the Angels chapter, I say yes. The more forms of meditation we can incorporate into our lives, the better, as the more you take care of yourself and others, the better taken care of everyone will be. I personally have always been guided in many different aspects of meditation by my spiritual guidance counselors.

The easiest way to begin any meditation is to find a place where you feel safe, warm, and secure—maybe a bedroom, a certain spot in the woods, or any area where you feel completely at home and in peace. Sit down in whatever pose that's comfortable and just let yourself breathe in, the blessings of your surroundings. Just be! Feel the oneness of your surroundings. You are connected to the Earth, the sky, the rocks, the trees, the water, truly everything. You are they, and they are you. Let yourself communicate your blessings to them, and they in turn will communicate their blessings to you.

Meditation is completely unique and individual. It is the formative grounding point in the foundation of our esoteric individuality and the spiritual energy of emotions flowing through your physical body. Tuning in to these emotions is how we become enlightened to listen to the messages of our Creator. These messages are how we speak to and talk with our guides in a more intuitive piece of understanding. We are getting to know ourselves better and in turn are getting to know them as well. We are following the path to universal connection and awareness by realizing it was within us all the time.

All the poems in this book were written in a form of meditation, in fact, the whole book was conceived of and written in a meditative state. Every aspect of enlightened spirituality on our beautiful planet earth teaches that we should remain in constant states of prayer and meditation. This is the elemental building block of awareness to a greater understanding of our creation.

I would love to share with you now some of the Study journal's more poignant pieces. Please enjoy as these are the very fabric of our beings that have been laid out for your perusal. I love each and every one of you and pray that these words will meet you in a state of love, grace, and hope, so we can all live out our greatest good and build a better and brighter future together in the oneness of our beautiful creation.

Meditation Artistic Impressions

1. The master of momentum - 1/28/20 - Gimel

2. Now expect to write the passage - 11/23/20 -Bet

3. As silent as the wind blows - 12/9/19 - Gimel

4. We know these rites of passion - 11/21/19 - Gimel

5. The fire brings foundation - 12/22/19 - Gimel

6. We sit here on sabbatical - 1/9/20 - Bet

7. A sense of just our shelter - 6/12/20 - Dalet

8. We dance in lines of vision - 11/25/19 - Gimel

9. With lack of only judgment - 11/25/19 - Bet

10. See just your Creator - 11/24/19 - Bet

The master of momentum,
has set about our path.
A crazy kind of concept,
between pure love and wrath.

There is a gentle feeling,
in the distance of a dream.
With visions of our outcome,
in a mindset so serene.

As quaintly as convergence,
of the clouds upon our skies.
We must accept reflection,
to drop our bitter lies.

And so the string before us,
is tied into the heart.
To eloquate the energy,
of dreams we must impart.

1/28/20
Gimel

Now expect to write the passage,
of the deeds we deem so wrong.
Wrap up all this judgment,
and send it out in song.

We stand far left of shelter,
from the warming rays of sun.
To speak of just an eloquence,
that's here by yet to come.

Now pry with hope and heartache,
on the gentle door of dawn.
As human we're indecent,
to hold that thought too long.

Yet here in fields of vision,
the curtain sheds away.
And wrought by only blessing,
We hear these words today.

11/23/20
Bet

As silent as the wind blows,
as simple as a sphere.
We see inside our searching,
what we want is always here.

It's called crucial contentment,
with who we are in life.
Living out our dream state,
eliminating strife.

We call on bright accordance ,
to coordinate our dreams.
To show the signs of vision,
of compassion so it seems.

Adrift upon distraction,
just a vision of our mind.
That all we balance equals,
to the goals we've yet to find.

12/9/19
Gimel

We know these rites of passion,
been through our bouts of pain.
We've sat upon the starburst,
which has become our brain.

Our sustenance is intrigue,
of the map about the way.
To open up the image,
of the thoughts we cannot say.

To bring them joy and sunlight,
as silent as the sky.
To watch their brilliant dazzle,
to see their reasons why.

We all have squandered moments,
in these memories of time.
Let us find these answers,
to a balanced life of rhyme.

11/21/19
Gimel

The fire brings foundation,
an element of hope.
That all may stand undaunted,
and find their way to cope.

We slip inside an echo,
of what begins a dream.
And give it salutation,
within the processed scream.

We've stepped upon a cloudburst,
to ride within the rain.
And dropped to distant places,
we've seen within our brain.

Now rolling down the mountaintop,
then sliding down the hill.
We quench the thirst of commonplace,
and right the wrongs of will.

12/22/19
Gimel

We sit here on sabbatical,
of life and limb and love.
Tempting these translations,
to one day rise above.

Lift within the smoke,
to speak of sight so true.
Where heaven has encountered,
the words they gift to you.

A logic of the lessons,
on a purity of path.
Has left us feeling breathless,
between pure love and wrath.

Now wrap within the shelter,
the illusions of our days.
And try to time this reference,
on these elemental ways.

1/9/20
Bet

A sense of just our shelter,
as a storm upon the night.
Now drifts inside a vision,
of a vast array of light.

With many hues of color,
in a vibratory hum.
We see a slight transition,
where all can see as one.

The purpose of this picture,
the passion of intent.
The prayers upon our whisper,
when truly heaven sent.

May leave us feeling breathless,
or energized in fact.
On mindful meditations,
to speak in truest tact.

6/12/20
Dalet

We dance in lines of vision,
a dual refractive glance.
Upon the wick of wisdom,
within the fires' dance.

A silent sphere from somewhere,
so close yet far away.
Has brought to us the mindset,
of what we've seen today.

Communicate compassion,
for all to understand.
Bring the weak ones with you,
lead them by the hand.

Strategic imperfections,
is just our human right.
Yet illuminate indifference,
to find what's good and right.

11/25/19
Gimel

With lack of only judgment,
we sit inside this space.
In lore of ancient concepts,
and dreams we must embrace.

Now passion brings us only,
just the distance of our mind.
And as our fingers tremble,
we see what we may find.

A mirror inside a candle,
a rock upon the way.
With balance and with vision,
now take this time to pray.

For all those lost to wander,
no goal upon their dreams.
We will for you the freedom,
to find your passions means.

11/25/19
Bet

See just your Creator,
in every rock and stone.
Sense divine serenity,
within your flesh and bone.

A conscious constant contact,
with what we see as light.
Will give us our serenity,
for what we know as right.

So open up your intrigue,
awareness if you will.
To find another moment,
of the passions we instill.

This spirit of a concept,
on a goal of distant dreams.
Which binds us all together,
to what it really means.

11/24/19
Bet

Inside of meditation the process of, *The Art of Eloquence,* is also about dimensional transference and elements of higher understanding, all of which can and will be achieved through constant states of prayer and meditation. You may have heard about auras, energies, even personal lights and colors. Many people who have psychic abilities are tuned in to what is called their sixth sense, this is simply a dimensional understanding. It is the process of individual meditations where each of us can attune ourselves to dimensions four, five, and six. These are the dimensions of communication, understanding, and awareness.

We are opening our belief system to encompass all that ever was and all which shall ever be. This is another aspect of universal source and the true beauty of infinite understanding. You are now seeing not only a clearer picture of individuality but also have incorporated a firmer foothold into the thoughts of these higher dimensions.

As humans, we are usually constrained to a limited understanding of our three-dimensional reality. Through a constant state of prayer and meditation, we unlock a pathway to universal consciousness. Let's play with that idea a bit, as there is so much more to learn, translate, and define on our pathway to understanding our communication with this divine awareness.

There are multiple aspects of the meditative mindset. It is within that mindset where we can access those higher dimensions of consciousness. We can literally form a picture in our mind, use that to build our intention, lead it to a point of awareness, or communication, and manifest that perception into our daily lives. As I stated above, psychics and empaths are already accessing the sixth dimension, and through deeper points of meditation, so can we.

You may be wondering how we got here talking about dimensions and realities. It has been the process of this book since the beginning. We are all awakening to a new level of spiritual understanding, and the dimensional comprehension has been laid out before us in a specific order, with intent, by our higher beings. Our angelic guides continue to talk to all of us daily through the elements of prayer and meditation. This is to be interpreted within an empathic awareness on the chord structure of emotional language. The reason being, that they are currently waiting for us to return commentary, from our side of this divine conversation. In my life, they have given me many insights and teachings, especially about the interpretation of this dimensional consciousness.

As humans, we walk in a physical state within dimensions one, two, and three, and that's how we exist in a three-dimensional reality. Dimensions four, five, and six are all about communication with the mysteries of energy or creation. In these dimensions, we connect with our angelic and spiritual guides on an emotional plane, which is why psychic awareness is referred to as a sixth sense; it is a sixth-dimensional understanding being interpreted through a conduit of divine energy such as a psychic medium. We are all psychic, empathic, and intuitive by nature. Here we are learning to tune into our perceptions inside of this awareness.

Having read this far through this book, we are developing a sense of individual spirituality through moments of personal realizations. The opening of dimensional understanding is no small feat. Not only have we been guided here by the humans around us, but we have been asked here by the beings of greater spiritual dimensions. Let your heart, mind, impulses, and ideals flow freely in the meditative mind. This is where our higher calling truly resonates. This is where we as individuals can live our greatest purpose while completing our human lessons and trials.

This is not a quantum leap we have just opened. It is simply an awareness of remembering our connection to the divine reality we were all born from and into. It is the connection of the infinite loop. There is always more understanding. There is always more light and truth. We are the infinity we are searching for. The arts of meditation teach us of our own inner truth. They are the building blocks of shadow work and brutal personal realizations that awaken us to direct our communications with the divine. From this point, we can finally open our minds and callings to higher points of understanding. We can literally branch out in any direction of thought—or in this case, theories about how life, the universe, and everything really works.

Chapter 8 Theories

(Thought-provoking communication of inward and outward knowledge and understanding)

We are all on a journey, a road, a path, of life. So here we stand beginning to realize, through the meditative mindset, that our spirits are truly theoretical beings born of energy and light equations. We are creations of a conceptual reality. The activation process of our spiritual understanding is much like watching a beautiful sunrise. Others can see this analogy in our lives, even if we may not seem to notice it at first. We are emerging to treat others with more respect and reverence through the base foundations we have built. We are beginning to see that every aspect of our surroundings reside within a complete oneness of creation and individuality. This stems from the personal premise of self-identity that was started at the dream state and built through meditation. Now we are ready to open to the theoretical aspects of how our creation, light, and energies really work.

There is a very thin, luminescent veil between us and the upper dimensions of our current understanding. We are here to rip that shroud open and interject thoughts and ideals into the mainstream of our conscious awareness. We are all individuals in essence born from the cosmic support system of energy and transfer. We are truly a conduit of divine creative energy. We both receive messages and give interpretations of divinity, much like a ray of light from the sun brings warmth, heat, and life-giving energy to all it touches. We now are that light giving warmth to all we see and connect with.

We have a firm grasp on the key elements which have brought balance to our lives. Without our conscious thought, this stability could not exist. Think about our reality for a moment. Understand how everything is held in that delicate balance, built on patterns, similar to a progressive mathematical equation. Know that your breath produces carbon dioxide, that the trees and grass breathe our breath and in return turn our carbon dioxide into oxygen, and the cycle repeats again. If this does not provide an example of the absolute oneness of our natural surroundings, tell me what else will?

I could speak theoretical analogies all day, yet we are here on a course. We have studied the aspects of awareness of our physical and spiritual realities through our initial understandings of the first six chapters, and we are now ready to speak about the theories of logic, creation, and understanding. This is the free-flowing conscious mind that we internalized in the meditation chapter.

Conscious theory and thought-provoking reality are the building blocks of this natural world. Through the first universal language spoken of in the chapter on Passion and using the arts of prayer and meditation. We are now ready to speak directly to the source of consciousness. I like to call that my Creator, as that is what this magnificent being has done for me.

Thinking theoretically is a much deeper and more involved format of the meditative mind. This is where we let the mind flow freely enough that it develops an understanding of the world, time, space, and energies that surround us. It is a composition of all these things rolled into one. Throughout this entire book there have been many references that we should remain in a constant state of prayer and meditation, yet not once has it been alluded to which one is best. Here's why: There is no best way to achieve prayer and meditation, as there are many paths to connect to our divine reality. There are literally millions of ways to achieve the deepest states of prayer and meditation. Fortunately for us we only have to figure out one.

We are all individual, and that is a universal truth. By raising our own vibrational awareness, we are raising the consciousness of all we see, touch, taste, or feel. When we pray, we are praying for not only our individual goals and desires yet also the blessings and care-takings of others. We are reaching out to spirit with our own unique care, compassion, and interpretation this is always returned to us in a constant flow of universal energy. We are built from this energy. Created by its passionate force of healing and devotion. Accessing our own individuality within this energy is how we can arrive at the point of achieving our greatest good. In this way, we begin an understanding of why we, as the person we are, signed our contract to exist in this exact space and time.

Every moment of our lives exists as a living point of

theoretical equation and energy transference. We are constantly in a state of thought and energy convergence with everything that surrounds us. That begs the question: What surrounds us? Literally everything. That is the only perfect and balanced answer. There are many people who engage in astral travel, time or dimensional meditations. We are as close to the upper dimensions of existence or the opposite end of the world as we allow our minds to be. How freeing it is to know that we can receive counsel from spiritual beings in a multi-dimensional reality. We can understand and give our blessings to the tree because we are, in essence, that tree. We can feel the water running through it. Take in and exhale its breath. Understand its thoughts and passions.

There are so many channeled poems of theoretical equations in the Study journals, from natural connections with the elements around us to speaking and learning from the animals, trees, rocks, and, of course, the living water which flows through us all. Please enjoy these poems. They have been selected for an activated reference to our theoretical minds. Let your mind wander; let your spirit soar. So much gratitude and love.

Theories Artistic Impressions

1. If you're looking for a theory - 5/12/20 - Hay

2. Talk to us in spirit - 11/19/19 - Bet

3. It's here we find the fashion - 5/27/20 - Vav

4. To work on transformation - 11/13/19 - Bet

5. No one will come to rescue - BB14

6. Together there is plenty - 12-20-20 - Bet

7. We've lit so many candles - 12/11/19 - Yod

8. In sulfur as in stardust - 1/7/20 - Zayin

9. Perceptive understanding - 5/17/20 - Gimel

10. So now we're given purpose - 11/18/19 - Hay

If you're looking for a theory,
of ritual or rite.
A pathway to develop,
a vast and bold insight.

Just let the mind go silent,
eyes opening to see.
The brilliance of the concept,
of pure divinity.

Now lift yourself to greatness,
as we open up our mind.
Teach your way to knowledge,
of the secrets you may find.

Brush the strokes of cipher,
you sense upon the air.
To realize your wisdoms,
were always meant to share.

5/12/20
Hay

Talk to us in spirit,
write upon your wall.
Vex us with your visions,
of another port of call.

We sit about in structure,
upon another page.
Giving time for wisdom,
in the curio of sage.

With elements abounding,
bringing just their light.
We draft another discourse,
in the sanctity of sight.

With love for all encountered,
inside our moments here.
We capture just our courage,
by exposing our true fear.

11/19/19
Bet

It's here we find the fashion,
just streaming from the stars.
Speaking out as rosebuds,
from Mercury to Mars.

As power lies in essence,
inside of empty space.
In a vacuum of the molecule,
which left without a trace.

So speak to me in torchlight,
let me touch your sky.
To see your dreams uplifting,
now teaching you to fly.

In moments of our mainstream,
we dance upon this stage,
In comedy and tragedy,
we write another page.

5/27/20
Vav

To work on transformation,
from sadness or from pain.
We must employ emotion,
from deep within our brain.

To seek an inner shelter,
where all we know is right.
To justify our reason,
and let our soul take flight.

Push your hard-built boundaries,
make sense of what you see.
Find courage in compassion,
reach out with empathy.

We sit in structured sentence,
Yet are free as beauty's bird.
When trimming out these fractions,
upon this written word.

11/13/19
Bet

No one will come to rescue,
the soul inside this sphere.
As none may come to witness,
boundless compassion here.

We sit in shades of silence,
and wash our sight with words.
To draw foregone conclusions,
that our song is that of birds'.

In passion sing to sunrise,
in romance, welcome night.
In truth between becoming,
their spirit gifts them flight.

We hear them dance so freely,
from dawn till after dark.
Their songs are that of wisdom,
now pray they make their mark.

With feathers born of freedom,
they ride upon the air.
With majesty unrivaled,
and no trace of despair.

BB 14

Together there is plenty,
apart there's just a few.
Conception of an afterthought,
that's coming into view.
Beside our insurrection,
of subjugated right.
We tempt to verse the sequence,
to find our soulful sight.
Equations of an echo,
the numbers in the trees.
The hound dogs of the hunter,
still the buzzing of the bees.
It stands to write the wisdom,
of the truth of deep desire.
It focuses on freedoms,
this spirit of our fire.
The elements of mystics,
stand balanced in their own.
They're reaching out with knowledge,
of how to lead us home.
Into a brighter concept,
of what we've always been.
A proverb wrought with patience,
stands in this pad and pen.
12/20/20
Bet

We've lit so many candles,
and burned the midnight oil.
To pray that just our future,
will never rot or spoil.

We sense a social cloudburst,
come streaming from the sky.
Here picking through these pieces,
to eloquate the why.

Now draft in silent stasis,
to give the sight a chance.
To fire up these fuel cells,
and live a light romance.

The tea now tastes of honey,
that a drone has brought to me.
We sip the cup so gently,
as we try to thank the bee.

12/11/19
Yod

In sulfur as in stardust,
on the singleness of space.
We sit here now to translate,
what the world tries to erase.

The concept of a theory,
of an interreladen dream.
A dazzling of dalliance,
in the silence of the stream.

In consciousness we wiggle,
a bit of here or there.
Yet on the other spectrum,
there is so much to share.

Now settled in this shelter,
with this passion's only thought.
To transform drafts of darkness,
into the light we've sought.

1/7/20
Zayin

Perceptive understanding,
to realize a sight.
To find within the fissures,
what makes it good or right.

We sit upon our distance,
to understand the dream.
To pause within the pretense,
of the universal scene.

This light is cast by angels,
now bask inside the glow.
To move forever onward,
is what we're meant to know.

So paint your point of purity,
in colors of your sky.
To spell your rhyme of reason,
in this calling out of why.

5/17/20
Gimel

So now we're given purpose,
a time to draft a dream.
A sweet dawn of transcription,
to another silent scene.

As the Earth may start to waver,
to tremble or to shake.
We could stave off indifference,
by becoming more awake.

An intellective mindset,
caught by visions of a goal.
To bring a proper template,
to illuminate the soul.

Wrought by iron passion,
cold and bent like steel.
These are those devices,
and to this plight we kneel.

11/18/19
Hay

Rolling along into the exit prose of the seventh stage of understanding: the communication form of our inter dimensional divinity. We have termed this as opening the power of theories. Theories are a way to understand specific events or happenings in our lives, and we are here to internalize how to make that work for us. Our personal theories come from observations and interpretations of specific events and natural structures of our balanced and harmonious environment. Now we begin to understand how to employ them as an element of our spiritual evolution.

Any dictionary will define the word theory as, "a well-substantiated explanation of an aspect of the natural world, which can contain laws, hypotheses, and facts." Therefore, understanding theories is not much more than an observation and explanation of how the world works. The great theoretical thinkers, philosophers, mathematicians, and knowers of our natural world are simply explaining what they see, feel, and interpret. Now, using our internalized understandings, so can we.

We know trees contain air, sunlight, water, and the nutrients of the Earth. Let us not only understand this yet feel it with the empathic natures we have built in our spiritual progression. We can see the power of the water moving in our mind's eye. Feel the support of the Earth as it guides the roots to stand tall, and understand the constant flows of breath and nutrition the tree is receiving and giving. This is a very basic parable of theoretical understanding.

If we build on top of the fundamentals laid out in the previous chapters, we can, in essence, see our relation to the tree, the grass, and all of our surroundings. At this point, we can not only understand their theoretical nuances yet we can begin to interpret their thoughts, feelings, and ideals. We can hear the wind as the breath moves in and out. See the sights that the tree would see and contemplate the thought process to embody it in our own understanding. In resolved mathematics, what we are now embarking on is taking these natural theories to the nth degree, the power of multiplying something in continuity by or within itself.

We are one with the whole universe. Grounded to this Earth

because we are the Earth and one with divinity because we are a piece of the great divine. Again, every ancient depiction of our human creation states, that we were fashioned from two individual things. The recipe for our human existence is one dose of the dust of the earth and one part of the breath of God. Through a continued opening of prayer and meditation, we realize the infinite potential of these conscious connections between our Earthly Mother and our Heavenly Father. Our hope, faith, and love are the balance we share with our surroundings on this physical vibrational plane. The more energy and light we give, the more we have yet to receive in this dynamic loop of understanding.

Through the foundation of the first six chapters, we can see, talk to, and receive counsel from our Creator, ancestors, and guides in what is now a seventh dimension of our reality. This is the original plane of their activated consciousness, the very beginning of their physical and metaphysical realities. Here, we are using our higher-self guidance to curate or eloquate the greatest good for all those we encounter.

Many people have accessed the sixth dimension of understanding. We see it in our daily lives as psychic intuitives, readers, pastors, spiritual guidance counselors, ascended masters of our history books, and the like. There are many people who see and talk to spirits or work on prayerful lessons, activations, or initiations. They then guide us in various sorts of deeply rooted spiritual endeavors. We are here to open this door for ourselves and to experience the true oneness of our own unique and divine human nature.

With these teachings laid out in specific order, we are engaging on a complete journey of understanding our personal spiritual intent and how that plays a vital role in communication— not only with ourselves yet still the physical and divine worlds around us. There was an old song and movement called "We Are the World." Yes, in fact, we are. We are not only the grounding divine energy of the world; we are built from the very fabric of universal wisdom. Artistic references often touch this plane of sixth and seventh-dimensional understanding. We are here not only sorting out the why of this, yet also beginning to engage that process in our daily lives. In this way, we can use it in our intentional communication with the great divine.

As an example of true artistic endeavors touching what I like to call creative source code knowledge, let's look at the author Dean Koontz. He wrote a novel in 1981 titled *The Eyes of Darkness*. In it and as he was writing this fictional representation. He wrote that, in a coming year, the world would be held hostage by a man-made virus released from the Wuhan area of China. Was this a book of philosophy or a fictional artistic endeavor? There are so many representations of forward-moving sight and understanding. Recalling the thoughts in the chapter on visions we can look at the prophetic words of our world religions, the writings of secular prophets, the speeches of spiritual figures, from across the globe and many more avenues of intuitively-guided references from our history.

This is where the meditative aspects of universal theories touch our hearts and minds, where we begin verbalizing or manifesting through prophetic or philosophical statements. We are opening our thoughts to the advanced concepts of balanced and rhythmical spiritual understandings.

As humans, we are filled with connection to the grounding forces of nature and the divine energy of spirit. We are truly on a guided and guarded path of ascension to the power of the light body. With the key inside the door to understanding the potential of our personal theories, we begin to appreciate that there is so much more to be thought of, internalized, communicated with, and understood. We have taken some wonderful and amazing steps on our journey and are now moving in the direction of communicating through the structured philosophies of our beautiful creation.

Chapter 8 Philosophies
(Personal creative communication on how nature, the world, and the universe flow)

It is here inside of theoretical thinking we question all that is, was, and ever shall be. We push the envelope, so to speak, as the envelope itself is a fluid structure of emotions or a natural evolution of growth and change inside of our daily lives. There are many differences between a theory and a philosophy. The first and fundamental variation is that a theory from the balanced spiritual mind is a comprehension of how the natural world works; whereas, a philosophy is more of a visionary process. It is an understanding or gnosis of what is to come for ourselves, our planet, and the many others we contact in the natural progression of our life path.

Dictionaries will define the word philosophy as "the study of ideas about knowledge, truth, the nature and meaning of life." Yes, in the definition of philosophy, it states that it is the study of the meaning of life. Here, we are using and defining this activation to become aware of our calling to communicate within and achieve our greatest good. It is in the state of intuitive philosophical guidance we can begin to term and actualize what our personal meaning of life is.

Our individual meaning of life or greatest good has been the core essence of this spiritual awakening process, so let's talk about what it means to engage our personal divinity and live our greatest good. It is a very fluid aspect of living in higher-self guidance and intuition. It means that we, as the individuals we are, can reach out with empathy and understanding to everything we see, touch, taste, and feel. It denotes enough belief in ourselves to guide and curate our personal wisdoms and thought processes to those in need of our enlightened foundational vibration. We can not only teach our strengths yet in turn can be taught by taking a long look at our weaknesses. It is a process of true equanimity and the aspect of personal humility. It is the recognition of individuality, coupled with, the activation of where we exist inside this stream of universal connectedness.

The universe itself is full of many wisdoms and laws, and it is in the state of philosophical thought process where we witness the awe-inspiring elements of its beauty and grace. We can visualize our understanding of the natural elements around us and, in turn, let them visualize us as the spiritual and divine being we are. While you may not be the center of the universe, know that that center resides inside of you. It resides in the core of every living and elemental being as well. Using the arts of meditation and theoretical guidance, we can visualize ourselves through the aspects of space, time, and knowledge. We are, in fact, a small piece of divine energy floating in a gravitational field, and wrapped in consciousness.

Philosophies are the fluid part of this spiritual consciousness. They are more than just personal; they are an amazing bearing in the wheel of universal manifestation. What we see, think, feel, and believe is exactly what is true for us and can be true for others. The more faith we have in something, the more foundation it receives in becoming an accurate representation of truth. Our words and thoughts are amazing tools inside of this forum. Written or spoken words and empathic thought and feeling are the key note structures of this universal understanding. We breathe life into our thoughts, ideals, and actions.

Using this as a tool, we truly create the realities around us by altering historical understandings or changing the course of coming events. In our natural settings, this can be seen like a river which cuts its bank away to give a clearer representation of itself inside of its environment thus recreating the environment in which it resides.

The guidance and awareness we receive when unlocking philosophies is like, that river, as a fountain or flood of information now being exchanged between us and our divine realities. We are accessing the codes and structures of our cosmos. Divinity is teaching us by speaking straight through us. By communicating and internalizing these understandings, we become a cleaner conduit of the divinity of universal source.

This is a dimensional understanding, an intuitive freedom of thought and expression. It is here in the eighth dimension of perception where we can use our spiritual gifts to see not only our lives yet what may be coming, going, or remaining in a state of rest or change. This is the place where visionaries such as Black Elk,

Nostradamus, Cayce, the many wonderful Biblical philosophers, and the great seerers, knowers, and teachers of our history engaged their wisdoms.

There are many philosophies in my personal journals. Be my guest to read and interpret these with your open mind and personal spiritual guidance. Check out the dates and see what terms may have already come about in the mainstream of our society. This book is a gift to all of our relations and each and every aspect was put here just for you. Enjoy it with blessings and prayers that we all can understand each other and find that common ground to growth and change. For the enlightenment and benefit of all.

Philosophies Artistic Impressions

1. The well has started rising - 1/2/20 - Bet

2. We put time on a pedestal - 11/21/19 - Dalet

3. Secure inside a vision - 6/13/20 - Bet

4. Now watch a sphere of amethyst - 11/4/19 - Bet

5. Now putting pen to paper - 12/28/19 - Vav

6. Bring back the ancient concepts - 1/15/20 - Dalet

7. Somewhere on rights of transcript - 11/29/19 - Chet

8. Sitting on a storm cloud - 2/9/20 - Dalet

9. Now stand inside the tempest - 12/24/19 - Vav

10. So here we praise the passion - 11/11/19 - Gimel

The well has started rising,
so far upon the night.
The brightness of its essence,
somehow transforms the sight.

Now sit on dew of roses,
inside of dragon's breath.
As the smoke it now imposes,
of what we are bereft.

A plague or silent scourge,
of many who still doubt.
That freedom of our essence,
is what this life's about.

Compassion wrought with kindness,
with an understanding love.
Will engage our truest fortress,
to the will of God above.

1/2/20
Bet

We put time on a pedestal,
in the prowess of our dreams.
To sit and watch unfolding,
evolution as its means.

The Earth it speaks its justice,
Mother Nature comes to call.
The sands and seas will rise up,
when hope it starts to fall.

So give your sight forever,
as long as it may take.
Guard your greed and envy,
before this future quake.

As nothing stops the sunrise,
lest the shade beneath the tree.
Our lives are yet as lucid,
as these sights we've come to see.

11/21/19
Dalet

Secure inside a vision,
alive upon a sight.
We see a certain someone,
to walk within our light.

A pathway born of freedom,
a picture of the soul.
A commonplace of intellect,
complete with divine goal.

The words now come from purpose,
a balance of the beam.
A process of awareness,
to yet is just a dream.

Enlighten us, Creator,
to the trueness of your way.
In philosophies of guidance,
we take this time to pray.

6/13/20
Bet

Now watch a sphere of amethyst,
refract its inner light.
Its purple hue of passion,
now romances the night.

A fire lights its orbit,
to illuminate inside.
The powers of its feelings,
in the cracks it cannot hide.

Such a simple daydream,
enormous as it's small.
The boundaries of compassion,
the door within the wall.

The here for and thereafter,
now once within our hand.
As we sit and gauge perfection,
of what our God has planned.

11/4/19
Bet

Now putting pen to paper,
yet not to write a book.
We're speaking of a mountain,
which once again has shook.

Foundations brought to ashes,
in the liquid form of time.
As dust begins to settle,
on every bordered line.

We watch the pen play fury,
just screaming out a name.
It tries to dissect distance,
from deep within the brain.

It says glory to Allah,
Amen and Bless'ed be.
It speaks in terms of love,
and brings our sight to see.

12/28/19
Vav

Bring back the ancient concepts,
of valor and romance.
A pure and simple daydream,
if only given chance.

Intimate is freedom,
ellipsing as the sun.
It binds us all together,
and shows how far we've come.

To find a new vibration,
that's just and true and right.
To internalize the energy,
on the pureness of the light.

It's elemental stasis,
in hues both blue and pink.
On brightness it will waiver,
yes, this is what I think.

1/15/20
Dalet

Somewhere on rights of transcript,
now scribe another thought.
To pen about a purpose,
upon a dream we've sought.

Within an ancient structure,
the seat begins to move.
As words fall to the pages,
like a wind that's found its groove.

A well of thought complexes,
these rainbows of the mind.
Its beauty once beholden,
within another's find.

Yet now it's drawn right to us,
to treasure it for sure.
Those beautiful resources,
are thoughts we can concur.

11/29/19
Chet

Sitting on a storm cloud,
elipsing only fear.
Has brought about translation,
of what's been started here.

A shelter to the subject,
in a unique brand of thought.
A tried-and-true transcription,
of what our sights have sought.

We lay upon the altar,
as the sunrise is our bed.
To draft and draw conclusion,
from the thoughts within our head.

In words about concurrence,
on this process of the pen.
We stabilize these talking points,
of just our inner Zen.

2/9/20
Dalet

Now stand inside the tempest,
on the drawing out of fear.
Within the hopeful courage,
that we will go on from here.

We're caught by just complexion,
on illusions of our gaze.
In silent introspection,
about our coming days.

So bright our ever after,
on decisions made from dreams.
We follow them in wisdom,
inside our ways and means.

With retro revolutions,
we can analyze the hue.
To better sense the future,
and bring our goals to view.

12/24/19
Vav

So here we praise the passion,
the draft of bitter dreams.
This sense of sensibility,
which sews us at the seams.

It talks about a discourse,
between our humankind.
It sets about the staging,
upon the great rewind.

We search for art and culture,
for meanings which subside.
The hunger of our essence,
we've tried so long to hide.

The heart it beats so quickly,
like it's pounding out the chest.
Please guide us now, Creator,
as you know what is best.

11/11/19
Gimel

Following the artistic impressions of philosophies, the balance and guidance of creative or universal source should again be pointed out—or at least looked at closely for the structure and counsel it presents. These artistic impressions, channeled through prayer and meditation, have dates on them. After that date is a numerical value written in Hebrew. This is the day and number sequence of the handwritten journals where this book and activation process originated from. *The Art of Eloquence* was truly handed to us by guiding angelic forces who are teaching us about the freedom and purity of our individual human spirit. Here in the philosophies chapter, we get to take a look at the hows and whys of this. Then we can begin to figure in things such as time, date, and sequence.

The first poem in this chapter was "1/2/20, Bet," the second piece written on the 2nd of January in 2020, two full months prior to the worldwide Covid lock-down. The third verse in it states, "A plague or silent scourge, of many who still doubt. That freedom of our essence, is what this life's about." There have been many artistic impressions of what we are currently facing in a global phenomenon. This is because in the true and fluid aspect of spirit, we can touch and sense divine interpretation or knowledge. This fluid aspect is what we have termed as "creative or universal source codes." It has always been the angelic desire of this work to take you to that place of understanding for yourself. The last piece of the Philosophies artistic impressions touches on a concept called *"The Great Rewind."* This is an equation that has gained much traction in my channeled theoretical guidance over the last couple years. Truly a gifted spiritual endeavor of social reconstruction, which will be looked at in depth in the fourth book of the Series of Divine Alchemy.

Angelic forces and creative source guide and bless our current three-dimensional existence, speaking to and teaching us through the auspices of passion, gratitude, and love. Here, we are learning how to connect to this language. A young mother once told me the first universal language of understanding couldn't be passion. She said that the first time she had felt a complete connection to universal love was when she held her newborn daughter for the first time. After acknowledging her beautiful connection to source, I said, "Yes, yet when was your daughter created, that was a passionate endeavor, and wasn't there an overwhelming sense of gratitude which accompanied that initial physical interaction?"

Inside this empathic language of vibration resides the universal energy field originally mentioned in the introduction. We are here gaining an understanding of how to access and interpret it and ourselves in a brighter and truer evolvement. The foundation of this awareness is an ever-growing light inside of us all. It stems from our passion to create the best for ourselves and others. The passion to love and care for those who love and care for us or to be understood and guided by those showing us understanding and guidance.

Philosophical enlightenment is a key element of this field. We have been reading this book as one piece or part of our physical and spiritual existence when, in fact, it comes from multiple and diverse aspects, each stage building a more complete foundation on the prior and for the next. What we are looking towards is not only the total understanding of the spiritual self yet the discernment, teachings, and guidance of the higher spiritual beings who walk with us and talk to us in our current existence. They exist right here in this plane of philosophical guidance and awareness. This dimension is where all of our spiritually guided, intuitive, and energetic information comes from.

There are many interpretations of the creative source code index. The truest thing to be said about any philosophical guidance is that it can be changed or altered by the aspect of free will. When we see our lives or our Earth heading down a dangerous path, we can and should redirect and refocus any negative or lower feelings of those interpretations. This way we can view them in their best and positive outcomes of light equations. This resounds with the mantra "Be the hope and change you want to see in the world," and is the direct correlation of why the angels have not only guided the writing of this book yet also put these words in your hands at this exact moment.

Our world and our Earth are currently facing a growing list of challenges. It is up to us, the spiritually aware individuals, to right the ship. To redirect the course of awakening on a much broader and bolder spectrum of existence. While it is true that we can only illuminate ourselves, that self-illumination process reflects into all our interactions. Once we have built our formative understanding of ourselves in the oneness of the infinite loop, anything becomes a possibility and everything is simply a point of understanding the intention and design.

There is so much out there to learn, teach, feel, and interpret. Throughout this book, we have built a natural resource of understanding how to communicate with ourselves, others, spiritually enlightened beings, and we have engaged one of the universal languages of passion. Here within the hues of theory and philosophy, we realize how much more is truly out there.

We have begun our communications within this dimensional space and time sequence. We have opened our minds to the absolute balance of our human existence, and now we are ready to start actively speaking our thoughts, theories, and philosophies to the universe around us. We are here to understand and believe not only in our abilities yet in everyone and everything that surrounds us. For that, we get to engage the second note of the universal chord of empathic communication. We are ready to pick up our tools and get to work speaking from the direct element of Gratitude.

Chapter 9 Gratitude
(How source creation works)

Gratitude as a tool for communication in our lives is a vital aspect of our spiritual progression. We have internalized the boldness of universal theories and philosophies, and now is the time for action. Acting, living, and communicating with all things in a grateful manner allows us to understand and witness everything from a balanced spiritual stance. Rather than bestowing judgment, we can reach out with empathy and understanding. Gratitude is how we wake up and greet each morning with a new renewal. Each sunrise is not only a chance at living out our personal best, yet a mission to follow the true direction of our higher self and spiritual guides. Each sunset is a chance to thank our spiritual self for living the very best of ourselves in each of our encounters. Gratitude is how we speak to the Creator with reverence and respect for what has been gifted to us in every moment.

Many times in our lives, we have been told that we must employ gratitude as a means of understanding or internalizing personal blessings. Throughout this book, we have engaged the balance of divinity from the personal and universal standpoint. We have begun to see where we fit inside the infinite loop and, more importantly, how to access these peaceful teachings and understandings. This communication, once like learning a foreign language, is now seeming simple and effortless, much like breathing in and out. That is where gratitude comes in. Gratitude is the breath of expression. It is time to be thankful for all our blessings and to convey our appreciation to the universe.

Gratitude is right here and right now in our spiritual activation process. That is because without the original foundation or understanding of self, we cannot truly express gratitude to all our surroundings. Without living in balance and harmony between nature, the Earth, and the universe as an entity, trying to employ gratitude comes off as a determination of will or ego. It looks like want or need rather than a joy or blessing. This is not what true gratitude is about. Rather, it is the fulfillment of the evolution of our natural states and abilities or our pleasure with the understanding and emotions of the balance and purity we notice in ourselves and others. It is the excitement of the full cup, the puppy dog dance when it sees its person. It is the chance synchronicity that makes our day brighter. It is that sacred space between breaths and the beautiful, life-giving air of our spiritual existence.

Gratitude is a thankful understanding of past, present, and future in points of memory and time. It can be challenging to be thankful for painful memories, such as a trauma or loss. Here is where we balance our spiritual selves and engage the understanding that this was the equation that built the foundation of our being. That we have a greater and broader perspective because of this experience in our lives. It has defined not only our purpose yet handed us our intention. Look at these lessons and be thankful that they have built the solid footing of the beautiful, balanced, and divine person that you are. Then we communicate that balance in everything we do. This is how we are truly allowed to express divine gratitude.

I once channeled a poem that stated, "How can we love the sunshine without the experience of rain." It is by doing the work inside of ourselves that we come to the understanding of how gratitude works and how to speak it and employ it as a piece of our daily lives. Using that as a reference point, we now understand feeling those deep loving and romantic moments may be the result of having first felt pain and loss. This is why gratitude is an imperative note on the communication chord of all creative endeavor and why it is sitting not only later yet right about in the middle of this pathway of speaking within our true selves to be at one with universal source. It is the root understanding of our spiritual communication within the divine dimensions of our current reality.

Gratitude is at the core of this universal understanding. It is the second of the three source code languages which will be employed in the pathway of engaging activation to living and communicating in our greatest good. Throughout the understanding and teachings of gratitude, we are thanking our Creator, not only for the blessings we receive yet also for the lessons that made us the beautiful and divine individual that we are.

There is so much to be said about the multiple aspects of

what it means to be grateful. The hope and promise of each breath, of each sunrise, of each moment where we can express love or give blessings to another. Through the aspects of gratitude, we can employ communication to the world or beings around us. Talk to the tree, the grass, the water. Thank it for being there to provide safety, shelter, food, or natural life giving resources to your already blessed day. This is how the universe speaks to us. Respond to it and see what happens. Picture the idea in your head of talking to a tree the way we would speak to an animal or baby. Speak from your emotions to the river that comes by to guide your way, or the open starlit sky, they are teaching us the true oneness of universal connection. These are a few points of communication within the elements of passion, gratitude, and love. Thank them for letting you be a piece or part of their divine reality.

There are so many channeled poems in the Study journals relating to gratitude as a root source of the language that enables communication between us and the great I Am. It is my privilege and honor to share some of these with you now. Please enjoy and let your gratitude flow like the river. Let it swim like the stars and float like the clouds. That is exactly where our hope and promise of building a brighter perspective on our human endeavors come from. As always blessings and prayers.

Gratitude Artistic Impressions

1. The universe vibration - 1/11/21 - Bet

2. Sitting on a moonbeam - 6/1/20 - Dalet

3. So sit inside your hourglass - 3/15/20 - Bet

4. We speak of nothing stellar - 5/12/20 - Gimel

5. We've tried to create beauty - BB9

6. So many times we've written - BB23

7. We're facing now the vision - 2/15/20 - Gimel

8. Listen for the answers - 5/30/20 - Dalet

9. Alas now built with balance - 5/12/20 - Dalet

10. Have you ever seen the prana - 5/12/20 - Vav

The universe vibration,
upon our shoulders lift.
To sense within the echo,
that all is true a gift.

To bring a brighter passage,
inside the light of day.
Or tune a timely rhythm,
upon our right of way.

The birds of song hold closest,
those dreams of true intent.
In playful passions beauty,
of how their lives are spent.

Now pray we find those moments,
to open up our soul.
And take all this creation,
to find its truest goal.

1/11/21
Bet

Sitting on a moonbeam,
sweet illuminated light.
Our senses start their stirring,
into the sacred night.

Revolving ever faster,
are these moments of the mind.
When words may never capture,
these thoughts we've left behind.

Grow with me in gratitude,
for what we have today.
The beauty of our blessings,
is the passion which we pray.

Stand now in the sunlight,
on the heartborn hue of dawn.
To thank the simple stardust,
for these tales we now yawn.

6/1/20
Dalet

So sit inside your hourglass,
take heed the time and space.
To draw into your mission,
the love of true embrace.

Embark upon the courtesy,
of those which are around.
And seek inside serenity,
the love which will abound.

Now open up the intrigue,
the magic of your mind.
The quantum of your caption,
to see what you may find.

Inside a distant teardrop,
upon another sun.
Our gift is grafting gratitude,
until our day is done.

3/15/20
Bet

We speak of nothing stellar,
intrinsic hopes and dreams.
Then write our way to wisdoms,
through mercy's ways and means.

We bring the self to balance,
through love and candlelight.
To pray about the picture,
in the sequence of our sight.

We open to the offer,
of what each day will bring.
To share the joys of process,
which build our hearts to sing.

Now pointing at the passion,
of the duty of our day.
We thank our truest teachers,
for guiding us this way.

5/12/20
Gimel

We've tried to create beauty,
yet from a humble way.
To extricate the ego,
and file it away.

To take the time for patience,
which wears forever thin.
To exact only effort,
with vigor and with vhim.

Our dusty hall now settles,
somewhere within the dream.
Our vision yet unaltered,
We flow the constant stream.

To passion and to kindness,
beneath the candles' light.
We'll move forever forward,
just to visualize this sight.

BB 9

So many times we've written,
of will and right and angst.
So many times we've pondered,
it's time to now give thanks.

To all the simple freedoms,
upon this unique life.
There is no need for suffering,
there is no sense of strife.

Enjoy your passion's progress,
stand fast your light desire.
With all we've come to reason,
let romance be your fire.

Now sit to pen the portrait.
of what this life shall be.
Inside the distant elements,
of thought that makes up we.

BB 23

We're facing now the vision,
of the dawning draft of dreams.
A simple slight incision,
on transition of the screams.

We broke the bonds of ego,
in humility the state.
To gain a just perspective,
of how we all relate.

So now we're sitting somewhere,
in the corners of our mind.
Perceiving all the symbols,
of the learning of our time.

Some may call this crazy,
yet here we are to say.
With gratitude we answer,
this is the only way.

2/15/20
Gimel

Listen for the answers,
upon your point of fear.
The joy and exaltation,
in the sorrow of your tear.

We're moving ever forward,
just to recognize the past.
To learn the simple lessons,
of the players in our cast.

We sit now in a palace,
of a rhythm cast in rhyme.
And speak about a pathway,
which led us here this time.

Through all our dear fruition,
on the sowing of our seeds.
We're here to thank Creator,
for granting us our needs.

5/30/20
Dalet

Alas now built with balance,
the structure of the sight.
The beauty of the basis,
of what we know is right.

We sit inside of shelter,
to reflect upon the day.
To count our many blessings,
in each and every way.

The process to perception,
is granted as a gift.
Yet can be learned as eloquence,
upon a timeless rift.

We bend not break this bounty,
to see it as a line.
A grateful word of wisdom,
now sits upon this rhyme.

5/12/20
Dalet

Have you ever seen the prana,
in a single blade of grass?
Or watched the blue-born pathway,
inside the looking glass?

Does structure touch sensation,
in all we hope to feel?
Will silent rays of sunlight,
cause damaged wounds to heal?

The audience is captive,
when brilliance is benign.
Yet senses deprivation,
when hope is left behind.

So run to kiss the sunrise,
to greet your dawn of day.
And thank the light for coming,
to warm your heart this way.

5/12/20
Vav

Looking at the aspect of gratitude as a language of the universe, it stands to reason that there is so much more emotion and understanding to learn and see within creation. There are an exponential number of truths and mysteries in this wonderful dimensional space called awareness. The basic three languages of emotion covered in this book are the foundation of a much bigger and broader comprehension. It is a language of empathy and understanding. What we are opening up to is the onset of spiritual wisdom, a connection to everything that is, was, and ever shall be. Think of passion, gratitude, and love as the primary colors of our empathetic palette. With their foundations, we can build the many grateful and graceful understandings of compassionate wisdom. We can feel the depths of the ocean, the height of the sky, and the expanse of this universal comprehension.

Many ancient philosophies stand in a harmonious oneness saying there are a great many mysteries known only in the eyes of our Creator. Within the platforms of emotional understanding, we open the discernment of what these mysteries actually may be. We can feel the depths of the ocean, see the height of the sky and understand the number and placement of the stars.

The first artistic impression was "the universe vibration," and stated that, "upon our shoulders lift." Our hopes, dreams, vibration, or energy are exactly what lifts the same in others. Literally everything is energy. When we transfer positive energy in the form of hope, joy, love, or gratitude, there is much more in retrospect that can and will flow directly back into us, our surroundings, and the universe as a whole. This is another example of the universal loop and cognitive awareness of how we can change it's course in our current thought patterns and time structures.

The second impression was, "so sit inside your hourglass." In the third verse, the quantum mind is referenced; that is the formation of self-identity. The understandings of theories, philosophies, spirituality, and balance all reside within a quantum field that is enveloped by our human mind. This fluctuating field is the focal point of divine wisdom and grace. It is right here inside of you. If you have heard the adage, "if you can dream it, it can be done," that is an absolute truth and the angelic building block of this book. The path we are on is to open this divine understanding and the energy that curates and binds it all together. The quantum field of the human mind is where our wisdom is engaged and a cumulative example of the power of this process.

In verse two of "so many times we've written," it states, "There is no need for suffering, there is no sense for strife." Having studied many forms of spirituality, I can tell you that one of my favorite teachings is the first elemental truth of Buddhism that states that in life, pain is inevitable, yet suffering is optional. The angels have a place where they can process their individual emotions when they feel overwhelmed.

The introduction of this book spoke about an early channeled poem that stated, "There is a castle on the hill where the angels come to cry." That is one of my earliest visions and a major reason why we are right here and right now. They, as the divine entities that they are, take their emotions to an individual location, seclude themselves, and allow the time to process properly before acting out in a misbegotten spiral of negative emotion. We can too. As we live our lives, there will be times of chaos, confusion, drama, and sometimes agonizing pain. Yet we as spiritually grounded and enlightened individuals do not have to wear that into our dealings with others. We can let it go to our Creator. Scream, cry, yell if you must, yet doing that in a healthy way in states of prayer and meditation is much better than taking it out on a coworker, innocent bystander, anyone or anything else. There is an end to this suffering, and we have found the way out by employing the aspects of gratitude for all our beautiful blessings.

In the third verse of "I'm facing now the vision," it talks about symbols. Literally everything is symbolic, this is an introduction to the divine aspects of sacred geometry. In meditation and visions, we are given visual references to see geometric shapes and structure. Again, if we study the writings of ancient teachers, we can see a lot of wisdom that has been passed down to our present culture. I recently had a conversation with a friend where we were talking about the Fibonacci sequence in art and culture. That is what still transposes to many modern-day modalities of art, especially into photography as the rule of thirds. I stated that it was between the teachings of Fibonacci and writings of Pythagoras that there were many universal truths. This is why we find that our human DNA structure is almost a direct representation of the double helix construction of a clear quartz stone and that our human fingerprint has much resemblance to the linear construction in the branches of a tree. Everything is connected in this quantum field and built upon a series of individual patterns. By employing gratitude and doing a little research, we can see and view these divine connections for ourselves.

In the final artistic impression "have you ever seen the prana," the word "prana" is a reference to the natural healing energies that the universe, the Earth, and any independent energetic being holds. This prana is the building block of hope, love and divinely created perfection. We can see this not only in the beautiful fields of grass yet also in the mirror when we see the wonder and spiritual balance in our own eyes. The last verse is a statement of gratitude, equating it with the light energies and vibrations that bind all this wonderful creation together. This reference is of unconditional gratitude for each new dawning day and thanking the light of understanding for coming to guide us.

Here, we are within so much gratitude, passion, love, and references to the building blocks not only of our society yet our universe as a whole. Sacred geometric structure through emotional understanding is that flow of energy; it is the foundation stone of all creative vitality, including the passion and presence of our Creator. It is here in the prism of light languages where we find that there is so much more wisdom woven into the very fabric of our beings. There are fields of the greenest grass, mountains, lakes, and rivers to traverse upon this path. We are ready to take an in-depth look at the beautiful building blocks of this communication sequence and see within our own element of understanding what our wonderful and inspiring creation is all about.

Chapter 10 Creation
(The building blocks of the creative universe)

So here we are at the beginning of the understanding of creation. Having been through theories and philosophies and having learned the universal languages of passion and gratitude, we can begin to look at how all of this creation comes to be. Not only where it comes from, yet how we as the individuals we are fit in and communicate with this divinely orchestrated plan.

The whole universe with all its teachings, understandings, wisdoms, and mysteries are, in fact, a true creative endeavor. We can see that in the similarities of source codes. This book was written to open the free-flowing mind to the understanding of their existence. Source codes are where the consciousness of the expanding universe defines its own shape and identity. It is where our Creator seeks guidance and counsel in our everyday attributes of spiritual, human, or metaphysical existence.

What I have been gifted is a way to channel that understanding. Creation is a beautiful labor of love gifted us by the Creator of our divine consciousness. We can look at any aspect of our DNA or physiological makeup and see the truth in the various aspects of our creation, across multiple faith bases, equates into one understanding. We are a divine creation born of the dust of the Earth and the breath of God.

We are created, in essence, not only to live our own divine understandings yet to serve. We are not necessarily a beast of burden yet a complete and divine individual, set about our path to understand and care for everyone and everything we encounter. To counsel and curate our understanding with each other and our divine beings. Through the earlier understanding of higher-self guidance, we are here to awaken each other. To remind each other what it is to be a growing light inside of this divine consciousness.

So what exactly is divine consciousness? What is this energetic field we have been talking about? Literally, it is the energy of everything around and within us. Everything we see, touch, taste, and feel is a part or piece of a reflection of the great and wonderful God-gifted light that resides within everything. We are all a simple reflection of a gift, hue, or shade of the color of that light. Now let's contemplate our gratitude for being a conscious entity wrapped in the loving arms of a vibrant stream of creative light. What a great gift we have been given.

The creative source field is a vibration or emanation of a power of life-force energy. The paths we get to follow in our daily lives are simply a direction and transference of that energy. Learning to use our inner spiritual and divine communication within this energy, to incorporate our greatest good, is always the proper place to be. Not only is our Creator the divine manifestor of our reality yet so are we. We walk the path of our daily lives touching everything around us. Simple tried-and-true creators of our own individual divine realities.

We are set in motion in this infinite loop of understanding, knowledge, learning, and creation to be artisans of our Earth. To take the beauty and grace of what we find around us and help it create more wondrous gifts for the next divine being that will be touched by this place's wonder and light refraction. The word artisan is a truth; each and every one of us touches the hearts and minds of everyone and everything around us. As an artisan of culture and understanding, we lay the building blocks for each other's understanding and learning as we walk in our daily routines.

Earlier in this book, I wrote about a poem I had channeled years ago, which will now be the fifth book in the Series of Divine Alchemy. It is named "*A Call to Arts.*" We are all God-gifted and divine creators in the future of understanding our human hope and love. We are here to lead and teach, guide, and counsel each other in our communications with the divine, and the Earth, as a whole.

There are so many aspects of creation to cover that one book may not be enough. That is the reason for this series, this comprehensive format of angelic teachings, activations, and guidance. The poetry shared with you here in this chapter touches on our formative building blocks of spirit and individuality, those that guide us all in our reflection of, or communication with this cosmic light.

Creation Artistic Impressions

1. We dip inside of fire - 11/28/19 - Gimel

2. We're sent here by discretion -12/24/19 - Zayin

3. A crystalline combustion - 12/30/19 - Dalet

4. Inside of our true brilliance - 1/29/20 - Gimel

5. A rock upon the altar - 1/8/20 - Gimel

6. Show to us the sunrise - 6/15/20 - Bet

7. Angels on the left of us - 6/15/20 - Dalet

8. The color of a corridor - 3/4/20 - Gimel

9. To open up our chakras - 4/15/20 - Gimel

10. An ego-driven raindrop - 6/9/20 - Gimel

We dip inside of fire,
the creation of the night.
In purposeful desire,
to a vast arrayed insight.

We've met another boundary,
now we're climbing up the wall.
To see what's in the garden,
as the summer slips to fall.

With all due passing intrigue,
we question why we're there.
Is it curiosity,
or some form of despair?

Seeing random flashes,
of the sky within our dreams.
We eloquate the mindset,
and believe in our true means.

Desire now for diction,
to say the words of will.
Pretending that it's fiction,
this call screams from the hill.

A long way left to travel,
to the joys upon these dreams.
The methods of the ancients,

pulse through our blood it seems.

Some days we watch the sunrise,
just waiting for the stars.
To find our mind has wandered,
to the sands of windblown Mars.

Now sit inside of freedom,
still trapped within this cage.
With instincts of survival,
we write another page.

The dawning of creation,
was all about romance.
These languages of love,
will one day give us chance.

11/28/19
Gimel

We're sent here by discretion,
on the wisdom of a whim.
To go about our vagrancy,
so far away from him.

Yet drawing ever closer,
we stand in sight and pray.
That once we will return,
on some ill-fated day.

While some may sleep in silence,
and some may dream in shade.
We open up to intrigue,
of how it all was made.

Now sift inside the vacuum,
on expanse of space and time.
To drop the sight of stardust,
in this reasoned rite of rhyme.

12/24/19
Zayin

A crystalline combustion,
upon a coming day.
Within a silent sunrise,
while we look the other way.

A filter of the fabric,
on an element of time.
Makes majesty the movement,
within the salty brine.

Allude to light and shadow,
the inert form of right.
The sanctity of substance,
upon this future sight.

With hope it can be altered,
in the strings of just true love.
As divinity in essence,
dreams not to push and shove.

12/30/19
Dalet

Inside of our true brilliance,
on the element of chance.
There is a piece of passion,
a place to sing and dance.

A joy of inner sunlight,
comes streaming from the cloud.
As we ponder silence,
yet speak not once aloud.

Diversity in destiny,
upon a single shade.
Concrete as certain structure,
to how it all was made.

Emotions of integrity,
a truth of inner will.
A master of the mystery,
stands simple to fulfill.

In thoughts of bitter balance,
on the triangle of time.
We contemplate our sequence,
in this myriad of rhyme.

1/29/20
Gimel

A rock upon the altar,
the sequence of the stone.
Which shines upon its brilliance,
the talents of its tone.

The blackness of its carbon,
marked by spots of white.
Shine within its substance,
a vast and pure insight.

Somewhere inside the system,
is the source of transfixed time.
We watch this standing structure,
of love and light and rhyme.

As simple is the process,
to open hearts of stone.
In grateful gifted passion,
that we are not alone.

1/8/20
Gimel

Show us to the sunrise,
upon your sacred sky.
Projecting a preponderance,
about your reasons why.

The beauty knocks us backwards,
as we step to see what's right.
The fires of foundation,
inside God-gifted light.

We hand to our Creator,
our love, our hopes, our dreams.
We try to carry forward,
through all these simple scenes.

A concentric circle,
builds the flower of our life.
As geometry is sequenced,
to create this end of strife.

6/15/20
Bet

Angels on the left of us,
behind our sight or view.
An open loving presence,
reminds us now of you.

With candles for creation,
and sticks of burning sand.
This vision for the present,
means love is now at hand.

Romantic as a raindrop,
a sweet concourse of dreams.
The echoes of the elements,
now sweep within these scenes.

An image of creation.
was handed us today.
On cause of our Creator,
please take my hand and pray.

6/15/20
Dalet

The color of a corridor,
with green and black and red.
Emanate from somewhere,
so deep within the head.

We're staring down our stressors,
careening through the hall.
In moments of our mischief,
we're writing on the wall.

So soft we see the vision,
with a straight and open gaze.
Surrounded by the intrigue,
of many golden rays.

To walk a path of purity,
into a distant goal.
To finalize fruition,
in vibrations of the soul.

3/4/20
Gimel

To open up our chakras,
or balance out the being.
To elevate our mindset,
or structure out the scene.

We speak in purest precept,
of a sunrise for the soul.
To see another vision,
of the passion of our goal.

The rocks are here for wisdom,
the sands they teach of time.
The candles light the way,
to write this thought in rhyme.

The solace of our structure,
will stand to just create.
From the joy we find in purpose,
for our mind to elevate.

4/15/20
Gimel

An ego-driven raindrop,
comes crashing to the ground.
It bends the blade of grass,
which never made a sound.

Divine and true by nature,
the grass it stands to see.
The rhythm of this rain,
its pure divinity.

On supple acts of kindness,
it permeates the earth.
As life it tends to generate,
through merriment and mirth.

In all it stands as essence,
beneath a bright blue sky.
When mists of simple raindrops,
teach us their reasons why.

6/9/20
Gimel

Expanding the mindset to encompass the understanding of creation—what exactly is that about? We have begun to understand the higher dimensions of theories and philosophies, and have internalized how gratitude and passion are two of the foundational bases of the universal language. Yet how can we grasp the entirety of creation as a concept?

Creation is within everything. Literally everything is a brainchild of either the Great Creator or a human endeavor. In human endeavors, there are noticeable patterns or formats. There are consistencies that continue to evolve in a scientific and analytical base of our understanding. This logic is a linear unfolding of patterns or events. It is the same with our great Creator. We have talked about sacred geometric structure and universal source codes. These are the patterns we can recognize to illuminate our minds to the aspects of creation as a whole, single, or infinite part of our meditative mindset. Throughout the artistic impressions, there are many thoughts regarding creation to be expounded upon. Again, asking for the guidance and graciousness of our loving Creator, I have been asked to share some of those insights with you.

In the first verse of "*Were sent here by discretion,*" it states that we are here to go about our vagrancy so far away from him. We have always been a part or piece of the Universal energy of light. We are drawn to this place through the aspects of time and dimension to open up and create our greatest good. We are here to give the Creator's understanding, compassion, and empathy to the world around us. We have decided to leave the light of conscious awareness and understanding to carry that peace to our loved ones. If you have heard the adage "we are simply trying to remember where we have come from," that is true. We come from the field of pure and complete compassion, understanding, and universal love. This is the Creator's cosmic light and vibration.

Verses 1 and 4 of "*A crystalline combustion,*" resounds as a bit prophetic. It talks about the end of our current time structure. The statement that our Creator is more of the Heavenly Father spoken of in the Essene or Biblical gospels. As that loving and compassionate Heavenly Father, there is sadness when discipline is necessitated for his children. Combustion refers to the

168

explosiveness, not only of our social structure yet still our creations and attempts to right the ship in a loving and positive environment. This is what the last verse states: That it is through our belief and hope that we can alter our current fear-based and manipulated time-line into one of love, compassion, understanding, and mercy. These are the true aspects of our creation and the gifts we are given to communicate within it.

"*A rock upon the altar*" is a description of the elements we bring to love our Creator with understanding. There are many people, including our spiritual guides, who believe in the unique vibrations of crystal energies. That is why there are many Biblical references to their use. This piece was channeled using a tower of nuummite, yet anything with a true elemental base can tell us of these teachings. We deserve a place to worship, to ground ourselves as the divine individuals that we are. We are free within creation to go about and do what is just, good, and right. That is because we are never alone. We have our angels, guides, ascended masters, elements, and even the Creator walking with us, talking with us, and protecting us everywhere we go.

Each of the pieces in the artistic impressions has so much to be learned from, discussed, and translated. There are light-code understandings in "*The color of a corridor*," elemental gratitude and prayer teachings in, "*Show to us the sunrise*," and "*To open up our chakras*." There is complete natural connection of emotion from the basic elemental platform in "*An ego-driven raindrop*." Then there are playful and intuitive understandings of creation in "*Angels on the left of us*."

"*We dip inside of fire*" was the first impression, and the last verse states that the dawning of creation was all about romance, passion being an equal derivative of romance is the first of our universal languages. It is through passion and romance that everything came to be a part of our creation. That includes you and me. We are truly a romantic and passionate endeavor of gifted understanding and amazing love brought here by the divine forces around us to continue in our own personal learning curve and illuminate others to a greater understanding of self and spirit.

There is so much more to learn, so many hopes and dreams, a plethora of balances and spiritual understandings. The more questions we answer, the more questions there are in front of us. There is an old saying from Rumi that states that the person who has all the answers has not been asked all the questions. While that is true, we still embark on pathways of greater understanding on a daily basis. It is up to us, the children of this great and divine light, to lead this charge for everyone.

It is here within the learnings of the mysteries of creation where we can look forward to bigger and brighter goals. To balance not only ourselves yet the world around us as a complete and divine entity. To treat everything with the love, care, and compassion that you so rightly deserve. Within these higher points of communication through self-awareness, we are ready to reach the pinnacle of understanding and tempt to find the healing natures inside of not only ourselves, yet all others. It is time to engage and communicate within those healing energies of our universal blessings.

Chapter 11 Healing
(Exploring your life lessons to accommodate all future endeavors)

After contemplating and communicating within all the aspects of creation, we arrive at the fundamental understanding that healing ourselves and others is what we were born to do. To create and curate many diverse infrastructures for everyone so we can help and heal. To put together the broken pieces. Seal the cracks and help our world become a stronger and more independent being in its entirety.

So what exactly is a healer, a light worker, a builder of future or forward thought processes? They can be many things. They can be the person who designs or builds buildings for people to make their dreams come true in or the person who took an extra minute to listen when we were feeling down and just needed to let it out. They can be a teacher who drops elemental wisdom in everyday references, a doctor who shows us how to process and alleviate our physical symptoms, or even a mystic who can lift and transmute heavy esoteric energies and communicate with spirit and divine beings. A healer can be anyone or anything which provides a feeling of hope or relief from any trauma or burden we carry.

Everyone can be and is a healer by design. We all have our own individual gifts and resources. We can all listen to and interpret what our friends and loved ones are going through. We each have innate spiritual gifts. It is through understanding our diversity we access that true strength to help and heal not only ourselves yet everyone and everything we encounter.

Within this book, we have uncovered a roadmap to the upper dimensions of communicating within conscious awareness. Healing is about communicating those thought processes in a healthy and uplifting manner. It is a way not only to engage our gratitude yet become the passionate beings we truly are when employing our greatest good. Learning to heal yourself, your traumas, your experiences, then using that knowledge to guide others through those similar challenges.

We all experience many learning curves in our lives. By getting through those challenges, we can touch others in a way that many would never understand. The true reason why this book is written as an open dialogue is that I need your understandings to heal as much as you are looking to my learnings for higher spiritual guidance and intuition. There have been many instances in life when we have all needed that deep emotional influx of healing or relief from physical or psychological traumas. Here in the eleventh dimension of communication is where we find that relief. We can pray, ask for guidance, meditate, listen to our angels and guides, let our higher beings comfort us, and come up with the answers we so rightly deserve.

As is with everything, healing is an energy transference. We have been learning how to open angelic understandings of the universe throughout this book. It is time we started employing that knowledge to open our own pathway to hope so we can heal and change the energies surrounding us. Remember the verse, "The universe vibration, upon our shoulders lift," this is true. If you can hope for change, you can see the change, you can embody the change, you are the change.

Everything being energy and transfer, we can view healing in many diverse elemental lights. There is vibration, awareness, physical manifestation of heavy or overwhelming emotions, and produced ailments of molecular impediments, such as a developed disease stemming from an underlying symptom (cause and effect), throughout our bodies. With all this being said, there are also miracles that occur on a daily basis in every aspect of our lives. So here we are expecting a miracle and getting ready for that to be a pleasant part of our very near future. We are a ray within the light of creation and the God-gifted miracle we so desperately need.

There are so many pieces in the Study journals regarding healing of different types and structures. Most of them have come from personal battles with loss and feelings of abandonment. When I look back at those experiences, I have learned to treat myself and others with the grace, forgiveness, and universal love we all deserve. Please enjoy these pieces on healing. May you find your own unique balance and individual guide to understanding.

Healing Artistic Impressions

1. A sentence born of silence - 1/21/20 - Bet

2. We write from pain and pretense - 5/5/20 - Bet

3. To hold a gentle wisdom - 7/16/20 - Gimel

4. To live upon a tragedy - 3/4/20 - Bet

5. A relative to intrigue - 3/28/20 - Vav

6. In hues of greenish pastures - 6/27/20 - Gimel

7. A draft of light transference - 6/6/20 - Gimel

8. On filtered rays of fabric - BB2

9. Observe the waivered echoes - 11/21/19 - Chet

10. In a palace made of parchment - 23/24/19 - Chet

A sentence born of silence,
on the altar we create.
To stick to planned perfection,
yes not to deviate.

The pathway starts to glisten,
as it heads up to the stars.
We trail on this teardrop,
from Mercury to Mars.

We've tripped our light fantastic,
watched truth succumb to vain.
On the founding hearts of hope,
to reveal just disdain.

As fate now falls behind us,
on the sunrise of our hope.
We find the true beginning,
in the ways we've come to cope.

1/21/20
Bet

We write from pain and pretense,
and learn as point of fact.
To visualize our actions,
yes not to just react.

Contrite, contrived, yet basic,
as simple as is sound.
We wave now to the distance,
with no one else around.

We search upon the sunrise,
through time and light of day.
To read the thoughts of ancients,
who come with us to pray.

To heal our Creator,
with love of life and hope.
Then greet the next great passage,
with thought we all can cope.

5/5/20
Bet

To hold a gentle wisdom,
or catch a starlit sky.
In time just out of sequence,
on the reasoning of why.

We drift upon a daydream,
to dance into the night.
To speak of purest beauty,
upon a distant sight.

The healing of a shadow,
we've heard of once before.
While knocking on the mantle,
of just an open door.

Now hail to awaken,
this truth within the soul.
To light the common knowledge,
of a long-awaited goal.

7/16/20
Gimel

To live upon a tragedy,
a comedy creates.
Within the lap of luxury,
a longing now relates.

In elements of kindness,
as gentle as the breeze.
With compassioned contemplation,
we pray upon our knees.

To thank our sweet surroundings,
for bringing us this day.
To speak of subtle wishes,
to laugh and sing and play.

A twisted, tied-up vision,
did once the heart impose.
Till prayer became our passion,
and love fell through the rose.

3/4/20
Bet

A relative to intrigue,
is the course upon a dream.
A shadow of a substance,
which only some have seen.

Still yet in separation,
from the horse which pulls the cart.
Now fixate on foundation,
from the rocks within the heart.

To climb another mountain,
and gaze upon the sight.
In passion of our purity,
to reach a new-found height.

Now read from just reaction,
of the lessons we have learned.
That dignity in essence,
is the bridge that some have burned.

3/28/20
Vav

In hues of greenish pastures,
amidst the dust and clay.
We seize another moment,
to express ourselves this way.

There's process to perspective,
upon our written time.
A word which falls so frequent,
in light recorded rhyme.

To see the well of wishes,
or guard the tree of life.
To realize that rosebuds,
could balance pain or strife.

To circle up confusion,
and infuse it with our peace.
Or guide those twisted tensions,
to the spot of their release.

6/27/20
Gimel

A draft of light transference,
now permeates the dark.
In meadows of the mountain,
that once were bare and stark.

To encapsulate creation,
of every rock and tree.
Then gaze upon the sunrise,
of pure divinity.

We purify our passions,
romance our hidden dreams.
To speak inside of vision,
and swim these conscious streams.

In tales of our torture,
or wantings of our will.
The time has come to rise up,
and truly climb this hill.

6/6/20
Gimel

On filtered rays of fabric,
ellipsing as the dawn.
We gauge upon the starlight,
just what we have done wrong.

We've sipped the dew of roses,
from the lips inside of fate.
And watched the rain bring newness,
to what we now create.

The pain inside the passion,
the tears behind the joy.
The birds which feed on freedom,
the words we must employ.

To carry out our timing,
or to realize our dreams.
And see upon this sunrise,
just what our duty means.

BB2

Observe the wavered echoes,
in the silence of the night.
Standfast, too, goals of vision,
on this sacredness of sight.

Believe in all your blessings,
to see the new desire.
Have patience with your kindness,
in the words that will transpire.

Keep writing out your wisdoms,
on each and every day.
And you will find the beauty,
in all you do and say.

And so a heart is breaking,
pray for it with love.
Help it find foundation,
to reach the stars above.

11/21/19
Chet

In a palace made of parchment,
in a gaze of blackest stone.
On a mesmerized misgiving,
of a heart of flesh and bone.

We continue in our conflict,
to the quest of purest truth.
To avail sight and order,
in the deepest dreams of youth.

Still set in our simplicity,
we bereave the barest sky.
To stand in deft duplicity,
upon our reasons why.

So open your due doorways,
in this sacrament of sound.
To find another fraction,
of love that's all around.

12/24/19
Chet

Healing is much like any other art form or creative endeavor. It is a necessary point of our spiritual journey, not only for ourselves but the earth and universe as a whole. Once we learn to engage this process as a daily routine and begin to eloquate our intentions to the world around us, a whole new shift of dimension opens to our higher-self discovery.

The earth, divine beings, friends, and relations all deserve our healing abilities to learn and grow, just as we are nourished by the produced nutrients of our natural surroundings. As healers by design, it is our calling to right this ship. To change the course from the malfeasant structures currently in place and bring about those aspects of growth, change, diversity, and unity for all of our creation. What a beautiful gift it is to be a part of the natural order of our current events. We can take this as a hopeful or joyful change rather than a limitation of internal freedom within our conscious thought and awareness.

We are here to dream, to create, to help, and to heal. We are alive at this time to usher in this great awareness of the divine aspects of conscious communication. This may sound like a daunting task, yet, in reality, it is quite simple. When we look at the pathway laid out in this book, we can see we are beginning the activation sequence of the light-body awareness. It is by raising this awareness we learn and teach each other in our daily tasks.

In conversing with all we encounter with gratitude and joy, I used to use the phrase, "I am puppy dog excited to see you." Be excited at every meeting and every chance encounter; live as an open doorway to intimate conversation and divine understanding. Once we can engage our empathic awareness and seal those cracked and broken pieces, we can use the tools of theory and philosophy to communicate with or guide the wholeness of the being back into a natural standpoint of balance and structure. It is much more about guiding into a completeness of original design, bringing back the purity of the unique divine creation and manifesting the understanding of its cause within the infinite loop.

Treat everything and everyone with dignity and grace, joy, and passion. Passion is an infinite feeling or endeavor to be the very best of all we can encompass. Let your inner energy flow within your own personal guidance and intuition. That way you can not only heal yourself yet understand the ways of using light and vibration to provide this awareness for others.

There are so many ailments in our current culture that are casualties of personal trauma or stress-related disorders. By releasing these energies through vibration, sound, light, or even therapy, we can alleviate most residual energies, which are those root causes. By performing the deep soul cleansing, the being becomes happy, safe, and secure to ground and protect itself from any other presenting factors of the original loss.

The Essene gospel of peace states that, "One may heal with justice, one may heal with herbs, one may heal with the wise word. Of all these this is the healing one. They who heal with the wise word, and this will most drive away sickness from the bodies of the faithful." Trust your gut; trust your instinct. We have opened a pathway to our divinely inspired intuitions. It is time to feel your way to the healing remedies of yourself and the many others that surround you.

I have worked for years with crystal energies and find them very useful tools to access deep parts of the energetic core of vibrational enrichment and balance. Visualize the root and see the light equations in the outcome of the therapy. Many people see auras. There are so many hues to energy, and we can visualize literally everything. Believe in your own innate ability to be the best you can possibly be and then do that. Find your own unique gifts and understandings. Raise the vibration not only of yourself yet in everyone and everything. It is with that in mind that I am reminded of the Hippocratic Oath, which so eloquently states that, "Above all, do no harm." Leave others and yourself in a better and more protected light than where you originally found them. Create and curate the natural and divine beauty of what it means to be free and whole within an autonomous and loving energy.

We literally are refractions and reflections of divine light. Be that light for yourself and others. Treat everything with the beauty, grace, and understanding you so rightly deserve to be treated with. That is how we as a culture evolve on our path to doing our greatest good. We are understanding so much about autonomy, equanimity, personal balance, and the individual vibrational integrity of our sacred and divine selves. Now we are ready to communicate within the truest essence of our beings. To drive to the core of understanding and intention. To see pathways line up amongst the stars. To talk to our Creator with passion and gratitude. We are ready to start speaking the third language of the chord of creation using our universal and life-giving love.

Chapter 12 Love
(The universal language and how to speak it)

So what exactly is love, and how is it one of three universal languages? Similar to the chapter on gratitude, love is an understanding of perfection by design. Everything under the guises of the Creator was designed in perfection and balance. Love is one of those perfect balances where we can communicate within that perfection.

Beautiful, peaceful, and loving energies permeate every naturally occurring element inside of our creation. It is all a gift; therefore, we can look on it with gratitude. It was all created from a passionate endeavor; therefore, we can feel the passion in everything we see, touch, and taste. From the oxygen we breathe to the water we drink, from the loving hearts of our families to the animals, trees, and rocks, everything is gifted to us and perfect in its timing and placement in our lives.

So how do we tell them how grateful we are for their blessings? It is not so hard to look in the eye of a flower, a beautiful tree, an infant, or even an animal and feel compassion. Sometimes, in our human existence, we get caught up in want, will, and ego. When we are in these distinctly human emotions, it can be hard to communicate within the divine guises of infinite love. We have to set our ideals and judgments aside and view the tree as its own independent being. See the animal as the perfect and unique entity it is, and treat the infant or any other people with the care and guidance we ourselves deserve to be treated with.

We are those infinite and divine beings that are constantly in communication with our angels, guides, and the Great Creator. We have come here to find that point of light vibration and transcendence to these higher realms of understanding. It is through learning to speak our individual language of love that our Creator recognizes our counsel or intention. Make your communications thoughtful and sincere. Gratitude not only for the good yet also for the hard lessons on your path goes a long way to achieving a greater perception of understanding love as a universal language.

Modern-day psychology teaches us that every person has different love languages. Yet the universe itself only has one. That is truly a peaceful and just understanding of individual representation, rather than our basic human understanding of want, will, and ego. The universe and our divine beings speak their love through care, compassion, and guidance. What is the color of a flower without its surroundings, and how do we view it both as separate and distinct? We witness it as unified and complete by its own placement in our natural setting. How do we become those artisans of understanding color, hue, texture, and energetic vibration? How do we guide or curate the flower to be the very best, most dynamic self it was intended to be? It is by opening the intention of impulse control we manipulate our surroundings to be comfortable, beautiful, or accommodating to the needs of ourselves and others. This is the same within the intentions of universal or divine source code energies. They are currently asking for our guidance, care, and compassion to right the ideological ship of our social misfortunes. We are here to help and heal by communicating within the aspects of our universal love.

We love in so many different ways. We can show love by dropping a smile to a stranger on our way to work, no matter how we are feeling. A kind smile or a warm hug go a long way to teach others that they are heard and understood. This is that genuine or nurturing care, compassion, and guidance of universal love manifested within our earthly creation. Our three-dimensional reality is our Creator's hug. It is that smile or understanding look that we see in the eyes of a true friend. What we are doing here is tempting to smile back.

Look with your understanding, and interpret with true compassion. How beautiful our current life cycles and spiritual awareness are. There are cosmic and universal source code teachings being passed down to us on a more frequent basis. Our current time-line seems to be speeding up, and we can greet each moment with this angelic care, compassion, and guidance. Hope and blessing are an everyday refuge. We are truly becoming more aware of cosmic energy, of global awareness, or, as I like to term it, the energy and light of universal source codes.

We are in a grounded state of activation into bodies made of light. Becoming independently more aware on a moment-by-moment basis of how we fit within this beautiful loop of structured infinity. We are walking on a path of understanding and communication with the divine energies that surround and permeate our structures. The angelic guidance of universal love is a key element of this greater and beautiful understanding.

Again, there are many poems from the Study journals that will shed some light into the elements of communication or interpretation within the emotion of universal and life-giving love. It is a completely autonomous language and has been set up for the understanding of all who choose to have an encounter with it. As stated in the introduction, let your mind wander, let your spirit soar. It is truly with passion, gratitude, and love that we get to share our individual experiences to balance the greater good of all human endeavors.

Love Artistic Impressions

1. To move in plane direction - 1/1/19 - Dalet

2. So stable is belonging - 11/28/19 - Bet

3. Now sitting in the shadows - 2/27/20 - Gimel

4. It's here we see the sunrise - 4/15/20 - Hay

5. To center up our structure - 4/19/20 Gimel

6. A sanctum of security - 6/7/20 - Dalet

7. We've written about roses - 4/16/20 - Tet

8. To sit in transformation - 6/27/20 - Bet

9. The universe is echoes - 1/1/21 - Bet

10. To all those cracked and broken - 4/19/20 - Bet

To move in plane direction,
embody it with light.
To speak within discretion,
of tried-and-true insight.
To gain a gift of knowledge,
and give it all away.
To teach a course for college,
in love and light and play.
Now see a sight translucent,
upon an open dream.
With vigor and with vibrance,
we eloquate the scene
We stand inside a doorway,
upon the great unknown.
To stare into the sequence,
of all these sights we're shown
So look here for tomorrow,
as the clouds they filter by.
Obstructed by injustice,
of the human question why
Engaging all the beauty,
of the colored hue of dawn.
Prepare inside this purpose,
for the sights we've yet to spawn.
Directing now the traffic,
on the element of fate.
To surmise just the tragedy,
of those who love to hate.

Unbridled is the concept,
that true love conquers all.
As yet it is our universe,
it's truly very small
A perfected piece of principle,
a drop of bluish blood.
A rainy day in shelter,
from torrents of the mud.
We set aside our madness,
in conception of this time.
As once it has been written,
inside a right of rhyme.
In futures yet to alter,
upon the dearest day.
We grow to love the passion,
of the universe this way
Where hope can shine like sunlight,
through the sight of open door.
Now contemplate this gratitude,
as who could ask for more?

1/1/19
Dalet

So stable is belonging,
to the balance of your right.
The truth upon your spirit,
within a great insight.

We waft on winds of wisdom,
on the echoes of the air.
To sense the love of beauty,
in all the sights we share.

The woodwork and the elements,
the powers of a dream.
The smoke upon the ashes,
within our sacred scene.

So simplify your structures,
let truth become your guide.
Find love inside the wisdoms,
of the insights that you hide.

11/28/19
Bet

Now sitting in the shadows,
we shade the light of day.
Bestowed within its blessings,
are love and time to say.

The moods about our magic,
the sights and sounds are clear.
The future brings fruition,
in the springtime of our year.

Alleviate your mindset,
stand strong and true and tall.
To build complete foundation,
through summer into fall.

Then well inside the winter,
building fires in the stove.
Take care those hearts with kindness,
within this blessed alcove.

2/27/20
Gimel

It's here we see the sunrise,
upon the new frontier.
While burning up the ashes,
of just our greatest fear.

We're shaking up our chakra,
and writing down the dream.
To open up the palace,
in the passion of this scene.

So here we are plum crazy,
about you, my dear friend.
A purity of romance,
a love that will not end.

When master meets the maker,
in a promise of true love.
This patient understanding,
now awaits you from above.

4/15/20
Hay

To center up our structure,
a top of broken dream.
To see the heart unwoven,
on the stitches of its seam.

We venture on majestic,
in the series of the soul.
To drink the dew of roses,
and continue toward the goal.

With light and hues of darkness,
a torch to guide the way.
Our breath moves ever onward,
in this and every day.

How simple is equation,
yet elusive is our love.
And still we're not complacent,
to search your skies above.

4/19/20
Gimel

A sanctum of security,
in creation of a dream.
A place to seek the sunrise,
which permeates the scene.

The setting is of beauty,
on hues of golden light.
The fires of our future,
encompassing the sight.

So find another fraction,
of just the distant sun.
Remember the vibration,
that teaches us we've won.

Now bring us back to basics,
to see how we have grown.
Then share this light with others,
of love we've truly known.

6/7/20
Dalet

We've written about roses,
encapsulating love.
And ridden winds of wisdom,
sent just from God above.

We've traversed many time frames,
inside the wave of life.
Yet not to find a partner,
or say I love you, wife.

Now married to this vision,
on the beauty of this time.
We structure out our passage,
in veins of simple rhyme.

This beauty is belonging,
to the hope within our dream.
Then magnify that romance,
to the universal scene.

4/16/20
Tet

To sit in transformation,
a cocoon of written time.
And evaluate the essence,
of the rhythm and the rhyme.

A brilliant affirmation,
of a longing love's embrace.
Brings focus to the clarity,
within this sacred space.

In dawns of just our daydreams,
or sequences of sight.
A conscious interaction,
of the time within our plight.

We sit inside the shadow,
of all we've ever seen.
To fix upon foundation,
the process of our dream.

6/27/20
Bet

The universe is echoes,
creation at the core.
The silent understanding,
that there is always more.

More hope than signs of chaos,
more balanced hues of dreams.
More love than just confusion,
more joy than there is screams.

Within this exultation,
we go about our day.
To drift upon the energy,
which greets us on our way.

Now soaking up the sunlight,
in the shadows of oneself.
Our prayers will toast the freedoms,
of hope, joy, love, and health.

1/1/21
Bet

To all those cracked and broken,
in the hallways of their mind.
To all the ones we've written,
who've left us far behind.

We sit within these pages,
on the process of our dream.
To elevate the mindset,
or vibrate through the scream.

As simple as our solitude,
upon the light of day.
We're hoping for your happiness,
and for this we will pray.

To friends and through Creator,
our relations one and all.
We pray you find the beauty,
in the passion of your call.

4/19/20
Bet

The balanced and rhythmical healing of universal love is seen and heard everywhere we go. In everything we see, in every moment we exist, in every breath we take, we are walking on a path of compassion, love, and understanding, not only of ourselves yet of everything we get to see and interpret in the deeper realities of our current being.

Love is an action word, more of a verb than a noun. It is where we get to show the other universal languages of passion and gratitude. We begin to see our lives as service oriented to help and heal. This is where we are truly speaking within universal love: saving the fallen bird with the broken wing, being there for a friend who is going through tough times, making sure a plant has the proper nourishment to grow and become vibrant. These are all aspects of the action of Universal love we get to show in our daily lives.

There have been so many instances where I have witnessed love as an action word. In the upper dimensions of spirit, we can see hope, guidance, and communication through thought patterns. We can hear the universal love of the shade tree put in our path to gift us freedom from the sun's heat on a hot summer's day. We can feel the cleansing of the water from the river.

As humans, we often tend to confuse love within our own manipulations of want, will, or ego. We try to say it should be this way or it has to be that way; whereas, love, itself, is a universal entity that binds us all to understanding ourselves within the everything. It is the infinite course of awareness, beauty, service, gratitude, and passion. We are that universal awareness. We are this great gift we have been searching for.

Reach out and engage through meditation, prayer, theory, and all the higher points of self-awareness with universal understanding. Walk with the love and peace we find inside the perfection of our truest human natures. We are not born from ego; we are born from universal love. A balanced gift of the Creator's elegant design. Let yourself live as that gift, that balance, that awareness of universal and life-giving love. The passion of a heartbeat, the gratitude of being understood, and the service of absolute love to each and everything we come in contact with. This is how we build our dreams, how we advance our society so we can employ our greatest good.

I have been so blessed in my life to have been shown the aspects of universal love and understanding, of self-awareness and service to our loved ones. This book is a natural evolution of that life-path awareness. There have been many tears, many trials, many elements of misunderstanding traumatic events, yet there were always the pure and divine aspects of understanding love. What a great gift it is to be treated with the balance of personal equanimity and willingness to learn resolution of our internal trials.

The angels are always with us from an early age, providing peace and understanding that our life is truly a path of awareness. We are here to study, guide, and teach each other in aspects of love and peace, to the awareness of light body activation. We are here to talk and walk towards the ascension of our spirits. The foundation stones of our infinity have very high vibrational elements and structure, so we are here to bring each other to a higher vibration to be one within this awareness.

There are so many spiritual texts that refer to the great mysteries of human endeavor. We are here to term and define the first of these great mysteries. This is the understanding of universal communication. Universal communication is more of a vibration than words. It is about action and intention rather than being the loudest. It may be true in our human understanding that the squeaky wheel gets the grease. In the upper dimensions of universal awareness, though, this is not the case. It is the brightest light that attracts the most awareness. God is light, vibration, awareness, universal love, and understanding.

So how do we get from here to there? How do we come from our basic human elements of want, will, and ego to access the upper dimensions of conscious awareness into that care, compassion, and guidance? We have started to learn the languages of communication with the divine. We have understandings of how passion, gratitude, and love are interpreted as action words, and we know the internal premises of thoughtful guidance and understanding of self through the dreams, visions, prayers, and deeper formats of meditation. So how do we tie it all together? How can we internalize the absolute freedom of our spiritual essences?

    We continue the journey of understanding. We write our own story. We engage our individual and personal language of life-giving love into the upper realms of this spiritual progression. We are ready to engage our own pathway to healing and understanding this wonderful gift of life. We are ready to understand the elements of the multiple courses to spiritual ascension for all living things. We are here to open up and see our personal pathways to the divine love, which is the core of our wondrous creation.

Chapter 13 Pathways
(opening your individual pathway to healing and spirituality)

It has been said that the farthest distance any person will travel is the one between the heart and the head. That is the basic integration of self and the quantum mind. By using the roadmap of this activation process, we can see that this distance is not so vast at all. We are one internally and becoming one inside infinity. That is the natural divine beauty of opening conscious communication and personal pathways of love and understanding within everything.

You are a complete and autonomous individual, wrapped in spirit and gifted with love, passion, and personal understanding from all of your life lessons, taking those understandings with you to the next level of consciousness and awareness. What a great gift it is, this understanding that each of us in their own inherent right gets to choose to be as free or as independent as they wish.

We can be free from pain, heartache, or suffering by choosing to live in the absolute joy, passion, love, and beauty of each passing moment. We are guided, we are connected, and that connection gives us the natural divinity of spirit we so rightly deserve. We are the singleness of open space and the infinite conclusion of grounded energy and divine wisdom.

For many years, I have termed the channeling of poetry, which I do, as interpreting the echoes of the winds. I implore you to engage your own elements of this, as we all hear different universal truths through multiple channels of thought, action, art, and activation. We are all given gifts by our Creator. This human life we are allowed to live is about finding that gift, tapping that internal well, engaging the amazing understanding which only you have, and gifting that to all. This falls back onto the mantra you have heard many times throughout this book and that is "living, speaking, and walking in your greatest good."

What is our greatest good? How do we know we are activating the height of understanding and awareness? This answer comes to us in the silent moments of our open mind. Through the arts of meditation, we are connected to universal source codes and can hear these yes or no answers. When you are in deeper meditative thought analysis you can not only see what you may have done wrong yet the best avenues to fix it, change it, or leave it be. There will always be room for apologies. In open communication with the universe, there are not only beautiful truths yet also hard lessons necessitated to encourage our individual life path awareness. You or the person deserving of your apology might just be here to learn this lesson, so please forgive each other for being human.

The individual divine pathway to opening our greatest good is an awareness and connection of the higher elements of spirituality moving through us. It is a connection to each and everything around us which comprises our physical, emotional and spiritual states of being. It is a flow between us and the energetic echoes of all.

Having heard many parables of what life may be, my absolute favorite is the river scenario. We are a course, a direction, a flow of both positive, life-giving resource and changing erosion technique building towards a future that is as of yet undetermined. Our natural course is one of gravity and polarity, moving with the changing elements and structure around us. We study these differing aspects of our conscious stream of emotion and events to determine how we will be running on any given day or time frame. Some days, we are gentle, moving freely and deeply in our course. Other days, there are waterfalls and rapids that permeate our mindset. There are deep pools where many multitudes of life, form and create their own identities, eventually connecting with other tributaries or bodies of water to flow our consciousness into the oceans of existence. We are the life giving water of spiritual existence and the grounding force of divine essence.

These channeled poems speak about the energetic exchange on the open pathway between us and the great divine. I love when people say they are looking for God. My usual answer is I didn't know God was hiding. Let your own pathway be enlightened in the celebration of your true creative essence. Let your divine communication of spirit be one within the balance of infinity and universal consciousness. Use your gifts and tools of philosophic thought and theories to understand not only your reality yet the realities of everything around you. Speak with love, gratitude, and passion with every living thing, and, as always, please enjoy these poems on your individual pathway to awareness and balance. A'ho.

Pathways Artistic Impressions

1. To say what lives and dies - 12/27/20 - Bet

2. So now there is a shelter - 12/2/19 - Dalet

3. So now we're cast to silence - 4/24/20 - Gimel

4. A breeze now blows from somewhere - 9/18/20 - Gimel

5. Vibrant is the echo - 2/1/20 - Gimel

6. We sit and drink the honey - 2/6/20 - Bet

7. An infinite surrounding - 5/5/20 - Gimel

8. So pay it now go forward - 5/6/20 - Bet

9. To become at once enlightened - 12/26/19 - Bet

10. Infinity in essence - 12/28/19 - Tet

To say what lives and dies,
or see the growth and change.
To open up the insight,
of which to rearrange.
To balance out belonging,
within a simple plea.
Find basic infrastructure,
in pure divinity.
We're writing on a cloud burst,
upon a purple sky.
The windstorm brings its wisdom,
to eloquate the why.
Here 'round about this corner,
compassion brings a tear.
Yet sense of understanding,
we have no thing to fear.
Our own conglomeration,
of memory and time.
A method of our travels,
in true concurrent rhyme.
We write the invitation,
for all who come to see.
Vibrations of awareness,
on our path to make us free.

12/27/20
Bet

So now there is a shelter,
a place of warmth and light.
A process of perception,
within our sacred sight.

We sit and draft a soundbite,
allusions of a wave.
With gravity and moonbeams,
in promises to save.

Adrift the open waters,
the light that leads the way.
We smite our oar sincere,
upon the sky of day.

To lift your name to freedom,
let passion be your guide.
Just pray within your process,
for truth we're not to hide.

12/2/19
Dalet

So now we're cast to silence,
to illuminate the light.
The will of just survival,
on the instinct of insight.

The palace of our vision,
so close upon the mind.
Has present ever after,
on this pathway we now find.

We're hopeful now in shelter,
in the process of this call.
That the peak of just proposal,
builds foundation for this wall.

We'll light the torch and candle,
for, ever all to see.
The brilliance of their blessings,
is the shade from just their tree.

4/24/20
Gimel

A breeze now blows from somewhere,
still not so far away.
It turns to give condolences,
for what it's knocked astray.
A wishful thought is pretense,
to chase a future dream.
A mountain makes a pasture,
from the tapping of its stream
Beyond the gold of sunrise,
up where the air is still.
There is no cause for ego,
there is no want or will
There is only slight vibration,
a vacuum made of sound.
A streaming flow of consciousness,
where love and faith abound
We're here to find the pathway,
to travel to and fro.
Inside these thoughts so distant,
we've places yet to go.

9/18/20
Gimel

Vibrant is the echo,
so long about the day.
With gratitude we realize,
our heart has come this way.

A bell begins to whistle,
somewhere so far from thee.
In time it will awaken,
the sight which sets us free.

We're sitting on the sunrise,
of just another space.
To leave behind a lantern,
a path to see the trace.

With angels of our apathy,
somewhere dispelled by fear.
We sit in bright becoming,
of the path we've started here.

2/1/20
Gimel

We sit and drink the honey,
upon this drop of dew.
A nectar of nutrition,
with colors red and blue.

Now forge into the fortress,
so deep within the mind.
And seek a simple answer,
to what this path may find.

Enshrouded by a sack cloth,
we wade into the sight.
And put it down on parchment,
as this we know is right.

To scale new abutments,
with the wind to fill our wings.
We're flying towards this future,
just as the heart it sings.

2/6/20

Bet

An infinite surrounding,
a fold of time and space.
A doorway to dimension,
may start with just a trace.

An element of nature,
the solid state of cloud.
The structure of a sentence,
of a proverb read aloud.

Now speak into the dawning,
of the dream we've come to see.
A pathway to a palace,
is a truth of destiny.

We open up the sunrise,
of this shade of tender time.
To tie it all together,
in a riddle of this rhyme.

5/5/20
Gimel

So pay it now go forward,
to pave the beaten path.
Illuminate the shadows,
which bring to mind your wrath.

A bright spot everlasting,
within the eyes to see.
As smoke within the fire,
of true infinity.

Now build your way through blessings,
in a moment of this time.
To saturate these tear ducts,
with illustrated rhyme.

We've come to ever after,
to see the present pause.
In just and due significance,
have faith now just because.

5/6/20
Bet

To become at once enlightened,
by a silent ray of light.
Encompassed by the heat,
of the darkest dreams of night.

Floating on a station,
of a boundless lack of fear.
Sounds of angels buzzing,
through sights of joy and tear.

We feel separation,
from the physical of time.
A unique exploration,
of our present boundary line.

So shaken by the freedom,
in the sight we now profess.
We drop to pray, Creator,
please guide us on this quest.

12/26/19
Bet

Infinity in essence,
is a rift of space and time.
As an elemental intrigue,
a dichotomy of line.

It dances on the distance,
it speaks to us in dreams.
Evolving as a substance,
it ellipses all these scenes.

So pray yourself the patience,
to open up your day.
And have your dream fulfilled,
in an actualizing way.

Surrender to the process,
which Creator handed you.
And have the strength of vision,
to walk this pathway through.

12/28/19
Tet

Everything is energy, transfer, and awareness. It is a gravitational or energetic push or pull, an ebb and flow of tide form and activation, wrapped in a light-bodied energetic consciousness. The river theory at the beginning of this chapter works so well to teach the use of life-form, cycle, or equation. We are the natural essence of spirituality. We are hues of divine consciousness. Think about the concept of the butterfly effect to see how everything is tied together in this spirit of understanding. We are all one consciousness, one energetic echo of the great divine.

In that concept there is nothing we cannot accomplish, conceive of, manifest, or build in the concurrent echoes of our spiritual or physical realities. If we can think it, it is already happening in our life path. This applies to physical and emotional healing, not only for ourselves yet everyone and everything around us. In the medical and scientific communities, this is called the placebo effect. The world around us is led by our example, so be the best example of healing, love, passion, gratitude, and understanding. If you want to see understanding and compassion from every living thing, then you get to be understanding and compassionate.

The higher channels of conscious thought are dimensional references to where and when our spirit is led to. Where are we going and what is happening around us? While we are viewing the world today, how do we stand as one within the everything while having and maintaining our own individual goals, concepts, and ideals? For this, we can start to picture ourselves in more than one aspect of our being.

We are small and frail, yet in conscious awareness, we are on a grand scale spectrum. Having done meditations that involve both travel and shifting of time and space, we can picture ourselves as so many different things. We are, in essence, a molecular structure, yet our energetic echoes are so vast and aware of all their surroundings. If we can visualize certain situations, then they can and will come to be a part of our realities.

When I first was attempting to access the understandings of universal love, I was deep in a meditative state using the Giant Body technique where we can visualize ourselves to be as big or as small as anything we can conceive of. In an earlier chapter, I used the analogy of an atom being the same process as our solar system when laid as a scale model next to each other. What is our universe other than a conglomeration of atomic structure and mass? When picturing ourselves as our giant spiritual, or esoteric, body of light, we can, in fact, show love to our Earth, solar system, and universe as a complete divine entity in the same manner we show compassion to our dearest friends. That is to supply the universe with our kindest, warmest and simple loving hug. Give it understanding and inspiration, a bit of your hope to carry forward on its own pathway of divinity and grace. This way, we are truly communicating our own individual essence within the everything. Here we can share our ideologies and manifestation techniques or just be one within this great and beautiful everything. We can understand the direction or flow of the universal languages of passion, gratitude and love. This is our own personal style of universal communication within cosmic awareness.

We can scale that model up or down at any time to see understandings from the natural elements around us. Think about a rock, tree, animal, or flower; they are already tied into the grand and small scale of cosmic awareness. They have already activated their individual light bodies, as they are born inside of divine understanding. We as humans come into this world with a built-in forgetfulness of what our true spirit forms look like. We are light and energy. We are understanding and consciousness. We are love, passion, and gratitude. We are intimate communication in the greatest aspects of that reference.

This individual pathway I have referenced is absolutely yours. No one else on the face of our planet has lived your life or has had your past experiences. We all come from a unique basis of understanding and intention. That is one of the most beautiful aspects of being human. Look at all this diversity with joy, wonder, grace, and understanding. Knowing that without those aspects of others, we in essence could not be the person we are. How freeing is it to allow ourselves the integrity to live in our own senses of conscious awareness, with the knowledge that everything is represented in its perfect place and time, that each individual entity was placed in our course to be guided by us and or we to be guided by their understandings?

Here in this book, is where a reference to a dear friend of mine should be made. My friend, much like myself, is quizzical and excited to understand the true secrets of our wonderful and beautiful world. One night, she couldn't sleep and was wondering about the aspects of infinity. She thought that there has to be natural representations in our physical world of such a grand symbol. Why would it permeate all cultures and involve itself in so many ways of our sacred geometric structure unless it was truly put here by the essence of divinity?

She opened many different world maps until she saw the ocean currents on NOAA's website. Then bingo! The universe is an infinite being, and tied to everything just like you and I. The ocean currents, that allow whales to communicate on a global spectrum, are running in the shape of infinity symbols. Our Earth understands this wonderful aspect of infinite blessing, now we can too.

There has been a great deal of angelically channeled messages and understanding spoken of here . We are activating our light bodies to communicate with the pure aspects of divinity and blessings. These are the true artistic natures of our human spirit and individuality. So what else is left on our course? What more can there be? In the nature of divinity and artistry, there is always more. More room for understanding, for learning, for growth and change into the very best of our human nature. We look forward with hope, light, and love, with conscious activation of our individuality and blessings. We are ready to learn about our own personal art forms of spirituality and understanding. It is time to engage the fourteenth element of our awareness and communicate within the truth of our teachings.

Chapter 14 Teachings
(Personal art forms of spirituality)

How does one begin the last chapter of a book such as this? There are so many more questions than answers, and that is the exact point. I recently heard a reference that God knows the things that I don't. When everything is energy and transfer, the messages of angelic influence are purely vibration and reason. They are echoes of design and elegance. These communication pathways are open to all who will build their own foundations with structure and intent. We are literally an antenna or conduit of divine energy. That is the root of all things.

Each point of light or refracted echo of awareness has a representation of inter dimensional transference. As alluded to before, we exist in multiple dimensions or areas of existence. We are here terming and defining what one of those aspects looks like to find that product as a balanced point. We desire it to equate, as all energy is grounded at some point in our three-dimensional existence. Where spirit is concerned, three dimensions do not find reference to balanced and grounded energy. There is simply free-floating energy and vibration. Mass or molecular structure is much different, as it is not constrained by weight, gravity, or atmospheric pressure.

Time as we see it cannot exist in this area, as infinity is truly energy and light. It is multiple hues, colors, shades and tangible assets of wisdom, truth, love, faith, and so much more. This is where our spirit guides and angels reside. In ancient spiritual literature, this is the difference between the words aeons and eons. An eon in older texts refers to a length of time, much like the word millennia; whereas, the word aeons would refer to levels of light or a dimensional structure which holds energy and vibration. The communication of our spiritual and divine beings is, therefore, very different from our human form. One thought process could stretch the boundaries of multiple universes. Quantum theory is nothing more than a basic understanding in these formats, more like a child's toy than a scientific endeavor.

The beautiful aspects of these upper dimensions of thought

is that we know enough to understand there is so much more to be aware of. Notice the simplicities, the connections, the nuances, and interjections, as the true beauty of this wonderful life. We can see these connections in every moment, from the falling leaves to the communications in our everyday conversations with our peers and loved ones. Everything truly is connected within these aspects of infinite emotional process and divine reference.

Divine beings communicate so differently than we do. We are here to find a way to listen to their wisdoms, laws, and teachings. Reaching out from within ourselves is the direct point of understanding necessitated to accomplish this task. Taking your heart, mind, evaluations, energies and going so deeply inside the oneness of your individual being that you can see the light of the forever that resides in your every thought and action. This is the true quantum of our spiritual, emotional, or esoteric make-up.

What is the light of forever inside your individual being? It truly is your own personal piece of universal or God given light. There are various literary representations of the light associated with what many have termed the Soul Star. It is truly a place rather than a thing. It is you. It is me. It is divine love, gratitude, and passion. When we feel things on a deeply emotional level, it comes as a vibration from the center of our chests and affects our whole being. That is because this is where the origin of our Soul Star resides. Our carbon-based bodies are the dust or clay of the Earth; whereas, our Soul Star or pranic light is that breath or wind of God.

It is the birthplace of all our emotional and spiritual endeavors. It gives us our intuitions and empathic abilities. There are many ways we use it as a feeling, an interjection, or even a point of reference to balance or carry our emotional stability. The divine and dimensional beings have learned the arts of communication from this sacred space of oneness inside infinity, and now so have we.

The very first time I remember seeing it being used as a way to show communication was attending my oldest brother's funeral when I was 9. It was an apparent light within the well of tears being choked back behind my fathers eyes. When we realize that there must be something more to this place, part, feeling, emotion, then we are on the right course to discerning and deciphering that universal plane of communication for ourselves.

What a great gift this life is with all the wonderful blessings that make up our individual realities. Each point, or term of endearment, or indifference, molds and shapes us into the beings we were born to become. How much freedom we get to experience in our own lives is a direct result of our life path and awareness. By becoming more aware of our individuality, we are freeing not only ourselves yet everyone around us to be the very best of themselves as well.

We have come from the start of dreams, visions, angels, prayers, and meditations, and here we are in the upper aspects of awakening the true divinity of our complete and balanced nature: speaking with passion, love, and gratitude in complete oneness with the universe as we get to watch it grow and change for the direct benefit of all we encounter. How beautiful you are for coming on this journey.

There are so many references of angelic teachings and understandings in the Study journals. It is with joy and honor we share some of these with you now. Writing is how I show love, and there is so much love flowing from the depth of our creation, that there may be only one avenue for culmination of this passion. One piece shared in the chapter on love states that, "Our beauty is belonging, to the hope within these dreams. And magnify this romance, to the universal scenes." Find your point of hope, love, teaching, and awareness—and above all, thank you so much just for being you, as you truly are the best and most wonderful you any of us could ever commune with on this beautiful planet Earth.

Teachings Artistic Impressions

1. To pride and greed and envy – 7/16/20 – Hay

2. Someday within the silence – 12/2/19 – Gimel

3. For reference we have research – 5/30/20 – Bet

4. Have we written yet a parable – 11/23/20 – Vav

5. To see inside the ego – 6/12/20 – Bet

6. To put it all together – 6/27/20 – Dalet

7. Now filter on the system – 12/24/19 – Bet

8. A dusky hue of sunrise – 1/7/20 Hay through Zayin

9. Now drawn to light the conscience – 7/6/20 – Gimel

10. To balance now our blessings – 3/3/20 – Bet

To pride and greed and envy,
or fear of structured wrath.
Yes, this is not our system,
it never was our path.

Enlightened by the blessings,
we see upon each day.
An open path to purity,
has come again our way.

We're gifted only logic,
created just by love.
From dust and clay and passion,
as starlight from above.

The wind gives breath its texture,
as Creator hands us soul.
It's ours to pick our purpose,
the free will of our goal.

7/16/20
Hay

Someday within the silence,
now expect our tongue be heard.
In driven contemplation,
within the written word.

We scribe about a future,
where many come to see.
A beautiful transcendence,
inside great mystery.

With vast, free-flowing wisdoms,
and discourses of thought.
A vision of utopia,
is what these sights have sought.

We learn from all our conflict,
yet passion reigns supreme.
Inside our gilded sunrise,
for once upon a dream.

12/2/19
Gimel

For reference we have research,
for words now hold the wind.
In echoes of belonging,
to start where we begin.

The process of a mindset,
on the elements of love.
With care and understanding,
of the path which leads above.

To draft now in the diction,
a place of perfect time.
To organize these visions,
into a thought of rhyme.

Now burning as the candle,
that is close upon our reach.
We search the ancient annals,
for the knowledge we must teach.

5/30/20
Bet

Have we written yet a parable,
a course on how to live?
A pathway to becoming,
just the gratitude we give.

In studies now of science,
or the alchemy of life.
We see in true creation,
there is no sense of strife.

Just calm and clearest concept,
of a vast and endless wave.
Where cresting is concurrent,
to the ways we will behave.

Find peace in all misfortune,
give gratitude to all.
Bring round this age of blessing,
with the passion of your call.

11/23/20
Vav

To see inside the ego,
a structured form of sight.
Or focus on the brilliance,
of rays and hues of light.

Vibration of a fractal,
we're left here now to see.
A shadow of an image,
within infinity.

Now swimming on the sunrise,
or flying through the bridge.
So far to destination,
yet here it is this ridge.

We step into this future,
with every breath we take.
So stop to smell the flowers,
left along for beauty's sake.

6/12/20
Bet

To put it all together,
or back within its place.
In dust of interaction,
or mercy of our grace.

A geode of dimension,
now breaks within our hand.
With pure and just intention.
of what Creator's planned.

An amethyst has impulse,
on visions of its dreams.
A sacred site geometry,
in process of its scenes.

Simplistic is the beauty,
of divine eternal light.
The vibratory humming,
on the path to pure insight.

6/27/20
Dalet

Now filter on the system,
of staring into space.
To open up our altitude,
with warm and soft embrace.

The mind observes an echo,
as it floats upon a cloud.
And tells us certain stories,
we hear its voice aloud.

Now drifting in our distance,
by now so far from home.
We thank our friend for meeting us,
as we are both alone.

Yet simple is the logic,
that here we are as one.
That we shall dream together,
until this time is done.

Then quickly as a heartbeat,
in a structured ray of light.
We are at once translucent,
off to another sight.

With brilliant bits of wisdom,
we once and both did share.
Connection carries forward,
as it has gone nowhere.

And particles of principles,
as does this truth remain.
That we are all enlightened,
if we open up our brain.

12/24/19
Bet

A dusky hue of sunrise,
bleeds through the tallest trees.
The bustling of daybreak,
now the buzzing of the bees.
We sit in slight transition,
on the element of time.
And tempt to move it forward,
in each and every rhyme.
Where is this understanding,
within this human realm?
To know it's in the castle,
on course at top of helm.
In reference of the ancients,
on the stories of the eve.
With a system left for spinning,
who would we be to leave?
Now setting out our sanctity,
in word or thought or deed.
Depend not on dimension,
as this is not your need.
Care and understanding,
empathy and love.
Traits of truest wisdom,
are calling from above.
Now heated in a prayer state,
desire drives us on.
To sit beside this pathway,
within this great beyond.

Our heart now flutters frequent,
so far away from you.
And time now falls forthcoming,
in this place within our view
In sulfur as in stardust,
on the singleness of space.
We sit here now to translate,
what the world tries to erase
The concept of a theory,
of an inter-laden dream.
A dazzling of dalliance,
in the silence of the stream
In consciousness we wiggle,
a bit of here or there.
Yet upon the other spectrum,
there is so much more to share.
Now settled in the shelter,
With our passions' only thought.
To transform drafts of darkness,
into the light we've sought
1/7/20
Zayin

Now drawn to light the conscience,
inside of the mind's eye.
To deliberate on diction,
in the sequence of the sky.

The clouds float by in purpose,
from the pressure they go forth.
And move about in freedom,
of east, south, west, and north.

They stop both rain and sunlight,
while still opening the same.
They show all hues of color,
giving rainbows their true name.

They walk both light and darkness,
sometimes they speak aloud.
What teaches us more lessons,
than to just observe a cloud.

7/6/20
Gimel

To balance now our blessings,
and keep them close to see.
We draft about their beauty,
as the path befalls on we.

To open up the doorway,
that none can seem to reach.
Then write it down as vision,
go on about and teach.

We tempt you now with triumph,
and sense your inner light.
Now gaze upon the spectacle,
of universal sight.

With customed curiosity,
we write from just the dream.
For all who give a listen,
about this sacred scene.

3/3/20
Bet

What have we learned throughout this sequence? What is our rationale or thought process? Has it changed or become further enlightened? Time is an infinite loop, and we are here looking more at the beginning than the end of things. The river of thought is now just becoming a conscious stream of awareness. The origin of dewdrops in our mountain meadows are just beginning to collect in the places where they make their stream evident to the world around them. Today, there is an open mind, an open sight, a new aspect of awareness of who we are and how we might have come to be here at this exact point in time.

We are gifted in spirit, searching our identities within the nature and nurture of everything. Now we have a roadmap to see it come to fruition in our personal spiritual and sacred endeavors. The true pathway I have been blessed to find continues to be laid out daily, as we are all just walking our visions toward an unknown future. There will be more in this future for all of us. I have seen both the beginnings and endings of our human time structures and can surely say that there is always room for more.

We are in the age of information. All our spiritual laws, insights, and rationales have been passed down over the many centuries of our human existence. We are here and now to right the ship of understanding and intention. The course to personal divinity resides absolutely within the individual. There is so much more inside of you than outside of you. Think about that the next time you are awestruck by the beauty of a starlit sky or gazing at the wonder of a mountain or an ocean. We can meditate on aspects of awareness inside of ourselves to the point where we are in another spectrum or dimension of light refraction and analysis. Yes, in fact, this is a gift from the God of the cosmos, and we are here to celebrate that.

The activation of the Merkaba light body is not only easy yet painless. In fact, it relieves all pains of trauma, stress, depression, and loss. Picture yourself wrapped in an orb of multiple rays and colors of universal light. What colors are your lights, and where are you currently residing within this universe? We are all in this together, so notice other bodies of light and forms of awareness around you. The river or conscious stream of energy wraps through all that we encounter. It is with the understanding of these blessings that we grow and evolve towards change, expansion, and enlightenment.

As mentioned before in this book, what a wonderful time it is to be a part of this world where we get to introduce the ever-evolving consciousness. We are on a pathway that leads us back to the places where we have been created. The great universal mysteries are here within our reach, and we are guiding our humanity towards them with beauty, grace, and balance. This is the true art of eloquence. That is the nature or meaning of creative endeavor, intimate divine communication, and comprehensive understanding of spiritual thought and theory.

As humans, we can touch all levels of conscious awareness and interaction. We can term ourselves psychic and intuitive because that is a simple doorway to understanding. All we have left to do is interpret that understanding, and we then grow within it. Have you ever had a feeling? A knowing deep inside that a place or event was or was not supposed to be happening for you? This is exactly what we acknowledge as we grow into those patterns of insight and understanding.

Not only are we all healers by design, yet we are all intuitive by nature. We are as free within ourselves as we are outside of ourselves. We are not only one and unified, yet we are still a part of everything around us. The angels speak to us daily, and we continually learn to listen. Sometimes when attempting to listen to a friend, it is best to restate their meaning and intent. When listening to your higher-self guidance, you can feel your way to these interpretations.

The original intention of this book was to take you on a tour of spiritually-guided visions and meditations. As the writing process progressed I heard that this work was to enlighten the spirit to the realm of possibilities, the infinite possibilities that we are all made of light and awareness. That it is through our own understanding and enlightenment that we get a chance to change, guide, or alter, the perceived courses of our current surroundings. Live with your love, with your joy, with your own individual sense of happiness and contentment. We are in this physical form for such a limited time, and it is true that we are all just walking each other home.

How does one end a book such as this? There, again, may only be one answer. That is, an understanding like this may never truly end. The thoughts and theories are infinite by their own design and shall continue to be updated and reanalyzed on a constant, continuous or moving basis. They are revolving like a wheel as a free-flowing point of energy and vibration. They are as much yours as they are mine, and we are all in this together. Let your mind wander, let your spirit soar. You are the captain of your own ship, your own course. You are the drop of dew that has been equated into the ever-flowing river of conscious awareness and the sole guide of your own destiny. Your lessons are so important to everyone, as they are an integral part of our complete life path awareness.

That is what universal source teaches on a daily basis.

Jeff Fosdick; The Fearless Poet

Summary

It's now we sing with blessing; it's here we heal with hope.
Through love of just this moment, where each of us can cope.
To hear within the future, the growing light of dreams.
And swim as just the water, within these conscious streams.

The *Art of Eloquence* is laid out as a pathway of understanding your innate angelic teachings and awareness. You are a healer, a light worker, an interpreter of spiritual or divine gifts within a multi-dimensional format. The activated sequence of our individual blessings has been laid out in a construct of multiple texts. These texts permeate our history books and scientific or metaphysical understandings. There is so much wisdom to be held within the pages of our history. It is by seeing the cycles of our past we can witness and transcend where we may be heading in the future of human endeavor. This is the reason we begin to communicate with our divine and inter dimensional guides: to right the ship, to place our awareness onto a new course of understanding with universal wisdom and grace.

Many people have asked me, in this work, for a course on working with energy or understanding light refraction. The editors I worked with were looking for definitions on how to pray or meditate. Still, the angels and guides who asked me to begin this work stated that it was to open the process of understanding that we are all divine beings and within that divinity is where we will complete these movements or structures of infinite reference. There are so many people who can teach us how to use light, crystals, heat, smoke, or any other point of energy as an activated awareness of divinity. *The Art of Eloquence* was designed to illuminate the aspect that you yourself are one of those great teachers. That it is by living in and understanding your innate connection to universal source that all this wisdom is available to you.

Within that connection to source, there is a great deal of responsibility. We are here to right the ship. To lead the greatest charge of our human history. Our divine beings have been throwing their proverbial hands up and are currently looking to us as to where to go and what to manifest in our three-dimensional environment. That is the reason why clear and distinct communication channels are necessitated at this point in our human history. Many people are witnessing the onset of conscious downloads or upgrades from the divine universal source. The course of this book and the enlightenment process is to define not only what those are about yet also how to communicate inside them and to give them the understanding they so rightly deserve.

The Series of Divine Alchemy will delve much further into the activation process of divine awareness. The formative building blocks of communication within the emotions of creation are here inside the pages of *The Art of Eloquence*. There is so much divine energy to be interpreted and responded to. It resides within every living thing. That is where we find the codes and structures of our scientific and spiritual awareness. In ancient or medieval spiritual texts, there are many instances of activation within fields of our energy and awareness. It is now time to look at these teachings and explore their many truths in our spiritual understandings.

The glossary of common terms, cited at the end of this text, speaks about and interprets a variety of these terms. Living in a light-bodied awareness is a beautiful truth of activating our individual Merkaba light. This was originally defined in the books of Enoch, which predated the original transcription of the Bible. If we look at our history, science and metaphysical literature, there is so much more to learn and interpret. Over the centuries, many people have convoluted these teachings to activate an agenda of manipulation and control. If you truly read the teachings of our great seers, knowers, and philosophers, they define the direct avenues to source code wisdom and the unwritten laws of God as independence and freedom.

The law is life, and we are alive, independent, and an ever-growing light inside of our Earthly and heavenly divinity. We are those great teachers and knowers. Our energy signature is exactly the same as anyone or anything else, and we realize so much more than we give ourselves credit for. That is the purpose of this Series of Divine Alchemy.

Here we are scratching the surface of a living, divine understanding that together we are so much more. The second book will be the energetic activation of our process. We will delve much deeper into the arts of meditation and awareness on a daily basis. We will greet each morning with a new renewal and each evening with a peaceful understanding of how to live and be one within our infinite loop and time structure. To gift ourselves these angelic and divine teachings of truth, mercy, love, and grace. Let us write. Let us read. Let us communicate within the pages of

The Book of Aleph.

The Series of Divine Alchemy
Glossary of common terms

In elements of understanding, many terms can be construed as relational in reference or at least substantive in use. For the properties and teachings of this work the following terms have been defined as such.

Activation;
>   The action of becoming aware of your unique spiritual self. It would be used as a verb defining the process of awakening to deeper personal understandings. Many people would also use the term initiation or epiphany for this. It defines the attunement of both physical and higher self to new levels of enlightenment.

Alchemy;
>   An inclusive term combining multiple faith bases and ideals. Historically used as a joining of metals or elements to produce copper, tin or various alloys. In this book, it is mainly used as the original conjunctive verb, to combine metaphysical or spiritual understanding and wisdom.

Angels;
>   An angel is a supernatural spiritual being who, according to various religions and spiritual teachings, is a servant to the Creator. Multiple faith bases depict angels as benevolent celestial intermediaries between the heavenly father and humanity. Other roles include protectors and guides for humans, the earthly mother and servants of God.

Ceremony;
>   A formal ritual or right performed in conjunction with divine guidance and understanding.

Codes (Light, Source, Activation, Creation);

Codes are messages from the universe, our spirit guides, or ancestors. It truly is an open communication within all the creation around you. They are an understandable language when referenced through empathy and the conversations we get to have with our earth, our god, our angels, or the natural elements in this current 3-dimensional existence.

Consciousness;
The aspect of being aware of the energy of internal and external thought in correlation with its unique and distinct surroundings.

Design;
Used as a verb, the word "design" is a pattern or development of lines, shapes, events or objects to build the foundation of a specific plan or intention.

Downloads;
The energy of universal understanding which comes to us at specific natural events such as eclipses and lunar or planetary risings or retrogrades. They can also be intuitive representations when we are undergoing heavy or severe emotional understandings such as personal loss, traumas, births or weddings.

Divinity;
The state or property of divine essence. The quality of being a divine being such as a god, goddess or angel.

Ellipse;
A term commonly found in the astronomical, scientific, and mathematics communities. In this work "Ellipse," or "Ellipses" is used mainly as a verb in creation coding sequences. It is cutting an oval shape at an oblique angle to arise at an altogether different point of creation or shedding away the past to make the future full

Eloquence;

A fluent, elegant or persuasive style of communication. Primarily the power of expressing strong emotions in striking and appropriate language.

Gnosis;

An inherent form of knowledge or transcendent insight within the aspect of spiritual, universal, or metaphysical truths.

God Light;

The light of pure energy and conscious formation which resides within everything. It is 100% creative force and individual identity, commonly used in fire or flames in ceremonies using candles. It also resides within the self, an individual's Soul star can be used as an active response to any situation we encounter.

Greatest good;

The achievement of our highest and best understanding. Allowing the individual to reach out with love, compassion, care, and empathy to all other people, places and aspects of our natural surroundings.

Light Body;

The easiest way to term the light body is as the Aura. It is the surrounding energy field or light of the individual. This is the place where the self and higher self come together, unite as one and balance our limitless potential with wisdom and understanding. Also see the following term, "Merkaba." The aura is an origin point of an activated Merkaba field.

Merkaba;

Originally a Hebrew word meaning vehicle, chariot or vessel. It is referenced in various books, of spiritual and historical adaptations, as being a multi-pointed, circular-shaped orb of colors of light which surrounds and encompasses the body allowing natural healing and travel through space, time and dimension.

Process;

An action or pattern of changes taking place in a definite and distinct manner.

Quantum Mind;

The quantum mind is the active force of our internal energy, coupled with the physical manifestation of our exterior movements and impulses. Not only is this a linear logic base, but also a supercomputer which evolves and grows with us on the path of integration of our many diverse understandings and beliefs.

Sacred Geometry;

Often referred to as the architecture of the universe, sacred geometry is the natural pattern, shape, design, and structure of creation as reflected by its individual symbols and meaning. It is the study of shapes, recurring patterns of physical representations and symbols which have deeply rooted spiritual intents and diverse energetic manifestations.

Sequence;

A linear order of succession in continuity of a series.

Soul Star;

A physical spot in each body where creation originated from. It resides at the center of the pranic tube between the Heart and Solar Plexus chakras, or right above the sternum, and can shine in multiple hues of color depending on what we are trying to create around us. Its basic representation is seen as the aura. It does, however, act as a catalyst in the Merkaba or Light body activation sequence.

Spirituality;

Spirituality involves the recognition, feeling, or sense of belief that there is something greater than ourselves, something more to being human than a basic sensory experience, and that the greater whole of which we all are a part of is cosmic or divine in nature.

The Study;
A physical room in my home. Set up as a place for meditation using dimensional vortex energy inside of a large crystal grid, it is complete with an altar desk and many different unique pieces of artwork and memorabilia crossing multiple faith bases and ideals. It is a truly beautiful place of spiritual alchemy where ceremonies can be designed and gifted to the earth, universe or individuals.

Universal Source;
The energy field which binds all points of light and matter together. A conscious piece of infinite understanding and limitless potential. The origin point of all creation, understanding and emotional endeavor.

Vibration;
The first element of motion and creation. In physics it is referred to as an oscillation of the parts of a fluid or an elastic solid whose equilibrium has been disturbed, or an electromagnetic wave. It is an impulse of energetic movement or flow.

A little gift

As you may have seen there were single verses in front of the preface, series introduction, beginning of the book, and the summary. These were all channeled as I began writing those individual parts. Here they are as one unified piece.
Just for you.

The Art of Eloquence

So now to tell the story, of how it came to be.
These universal teachings, so deep inside of me.
Listen to the echoes, the wisdom of the wind.
Inside this truth and light, it's here we now begin.

To hear the ancient teachings, as a whisper on the air.
To balance out these echoes and bring them all to bare.
Now introduce the system of what we see as life,
to find the fledgling feelings, which build our joy from strife.

To communicate with oneness, in everything and all.
To bring about the balance, of great and very small.
In the micro and the macro, hear the angels in the air.
As guide and guard and witness to what we now will share.

It's now we sing with blessing, it's here we heal with hope.
Through love of just this moment, where each of us can cope.
To hear within the future, the growing light of dreams.
And swim as just the water, within these conscious streams.

Jeff
The Fearless Poet

The back pages of this book are meant for your notes, annotations or questions. I implore each and everyone who reads this text to reach out to me and ask or comment anything they wish. Write it down here, I am waiting to hear your thoughts.
Jeff